Cartels

Cartels

Challenge to a Free World

By

WENDELL BERGE

Assistant Attorney General
of the United States

BeardBooks
Washington, D.C.

Reprinted 2000 by Beard Books, Washington, D.C.

ISBN 1-58798-013-4

Printed in the United States of America

Preface

The end of the war will find us on the threshold of the greatest technical and scientific developments in history. Light metals, plastics, television, new chemical and electrical techniques are but a few of the instruments which will furnish the stuff for the pioneers of a new age. The challenge of housing will excite bold minds to action, on a scale never before attempted, to wipe out slums and give dwellers in country and city alike a new and higher standard of living. Not only at home, but also abroad, the opportunities for daring enterprise which will be offered by the needs of world reconstruction will surpass anything ever before known.

How are we going to meet this challenge? At the outset, we must face frankly the greatest obstacle to making the most of our opportunity It is the threat of cartel control of major world industries. Unless this threat is understood and dealt with decisively, our opportunity to realize the great potential benefits of a free economy will be lost. And worse still, the hope of maintaining democratic political institutions will be seriously impaired.

The pattern of cartel operations has been clearly revealed in recent years by antitrust investigations. From public records in antitrust proceedings and congressional hearings, information about cartel operations is now available. The public should be familiar with the facts. As head of the Antitrust Division of the Department of Justice, I have frequently been called upon to discuss cartel problems before congressional committees, trade associations and civic groups. Since my testimony and speeches received varying degrees of public notice at the time they were given, the casual reader of newspaper reports necessarily obtained only an impressionistic picture of the far-flung ramifications of the subject. Something more is needed for thorough understanding.

With this thought in mind, a number of friends and associates have suggested from time to time that my material should be woven together in book form. This I have undertaken to do in the present volume.

Merely to make assertions about the evil effect of cartels is a simple matter. But I believe that the real usefulness of this book will depend upon its fairly detailed explanation of the operation of particular cartels, with direct quotations from letters, memoranda and other documents.

While I have not tried to compile a complete source-book, I have striven to make this discussion as non-technical as possible. The factual material is drawn largely from the documents of the Kilgore, Truman and Bone Senate Committees, and from the public records of antitrust cases.

The investigations which unearthed the facts cited in this book were, of course, the work of a great many men and women in the Antitrust Division extending over a period of years. Acknowledgment of credit to all of them would be impossible. Many of the men who have developed these facts are now serving their country in the armed forces.

I cannot praise too highly the ability, energy and devotion to public service of the men and women of the Antitrust Division. It is a privilege to head such a splendid staff, as it is to serve under such an able and distinguished Attorney General as

Francis Biddle, who has maintained at all times an extremely deep interest in our cartel work and has given it his fullest support. Attorney General Biddle has repeatedly impressed upon me his own conviction that the vigorous enforcement of the antitrust laws against cartels is an indispensable condition to the maintenance of a free competitive economy in this country.

In the preparation of this book I am particularly indebted to Joseph Borkin of my staff, who is in my opinion one of the best informed men in America on the activities of international cartels. For more than five years Mr. Borkin has devoted his great resourcefulness and energy to investigation and study of cartel problems. His contribution in this field has been invaluable.

I also want to acknowledge my deep obligation to my First Assistant, Edward H. Levi, with whom I have spent many hours discussing the legal and economic problems of cartels, and on whom I have relied so heavily in the practical administration of the Antitrust Division. And I am greatly indebted to Myron W. Watkins, Charles A. Welsh, Ernest S. Meyers, George P. Comer, Herbert A. Berman, Bartholomew Diggins, Robert Hunter, and Heinrich Kronstein of the Antitrust Division staff, all of whom have been of great assistance in the preparation of this book and in the cartel work of the Division. Professor Walton Hamilton of Yale, who has been a part-time member of the staff, has also worked closely with me on these matters and has made a signal contribution to our work.

Mr. M. B. Schnapper, Executive Secretary of the American Council of Public Affairs, has been of greatest assistance in the planning of this book and in the editorial work which it has involved.

WENDELL BERGE

CONTENTS

1
Trusts to Cartels

The problem of monopoly is no longer a distinctively domestic and national phenomenon. It has come to encompass the whole world. Like a parasite on its host, monopoly has grown with the marketplace. Today hardly a corner of the world remains free from the malignant influence of its latest and most sinister form, the cartel. Diamonds discovered in Arkansas may prompt agitated conferences within 48 hours in London and the Belgian Congo; a lawsuit in New York challenging the aluminum monopoly brings simultaneous outbursts of oratory in the House of Lords and of vituperation on the Axis radio.

For over half a century, the Sherman Act has stood as a positive expression of the inflexible will of the American people to preserve freedom of economic opportunity. When this measure was enacted the oil, whiskey, and sugar trusts had placed barriers directly athwart the arteries of commerce and were exacting tolls for every gallon or pound of product permitted to pass. Since nation-wide industrial monopoly of a comparatively stable character first took the form of a simple trust agreement the Sherman Act came to be designated an antitrust statute. But its thrust was positive: the maintenance of free, competitive markets and a democratic system of industrial control.

If such an Act were passed today, I am quite sure it would be called an "Anti-Cartel Act." For our attention is at the present time focused on industrial monopoly in a different form, operating in a wider orbit. But our basic concern is the same. We are as determined today as were our grandfathers two generations ago—indeed, as were the founders of the republic—to countenance no infringement of the right to engage in any legitimate enterprise and to conduct business without let or hindrance from any self-constituted group presuming to monopolize trade or industry.

The Sherman Act has proved an effective instrument no less for dealing with the cartel problem than for curbing the trusts. It must be conceded, however, that, in default of proper implementation and appropriate supplementation, it has not fully realized the salutary object for which it was designed. In particular, our policies with regard to patents, trademarks, the tariff, monetary and credit matters, interstate commerce, and foreign trade, all have a direct bearing upon competition and the pattern of industrial organization. They are important factors conditioning the efficacy of a free market for performing its basic economic functions. To our comparative neglect of the incidence of these policies on the problem of maintaining healthful competitive conditions in industry must be attributed a large share of the responsibility for the difference between anti-trust policies and business practice.

In these circumstances, cartels—which, in effect, are trusts magnified to an international scale—have been able by clandestine means to impress their sinister mark upon our economy. In mobilizing for war, we discovered, almost too late, that they were responsible for shortage after shortage of vital materials.

The fact is that they have retarded technological advance and the introduction of improved devices and products whenever such developments seemed to threaten their vested interests despite the fact that thereby national security might be jeopardized. They have, indeed, obstructed and in no small measure thwarted the declared foreign policies of the American government, placing their own business interests above the public interests.

In peace time, their high-price, restricted-output strategy has impeded the advance of our living standards and general economic well-being. Through the abuse of our patent system, cartel controls have been established over large segments of technology. With this leverage, industrial monopolies of international compass have at times deliberately brought about the deterioration of quality standards. When it might be to their advantage in maintaining or exploiting their monopoly position, they have adulterated their products to an extent and in a manner endangering the health, and even the lives, of consumers. Almost incredible as these assertions may be, they are not subject to contradiction—the incontrovertible facts are clearly set forth in Congressional investigations and in the evidence in antitrust cases of the Department of Justice.

Cartels are in essence private governments which threaten to subvert and even engulf duly constituted authority. In Germany, Kaiserism and later Nazism received enormous impetus, indeed decisive support, from the regimented, cartelized structure of the national economy.

Totalitarianism represents simply the ultimate consummation of cartelism—the final, full expression of the reactionary forces stemming from special privilege. In totalitarian states all industrial enterprise is subservient to the predatory interests and fear-dominated will of a government which openly flouts the democratic principle of consent of the governed. In the economic sphere, the investment of fresh capital, the volume of production, the prices to be charged, the markets to be served, are determined by arbitrary decrees. Risk-taking, managerial discretion, bargaining freedom, the essential elements of the capitalistic system as we have known it, are absent. One can neither start a new industry, launch a new enterprise, or change one's occupation without first obtaining official consent. It is in the nature of cartels that they should operate in a similar fashion, even if in their application the devices used for consolidating the vested interests of established concerns and throttling the dynamic forces which economic freedom would release may lack something of the rigor they exhibit under totalitarian "leadership." In order to maintain their control over production and prices cartels must determine who may enter the industry, how they shall operate and where they may sell.

The basic American concept of free enterprise is the antithesis of a cartelized market. Yet, all too frequently, some of our industrialists have had the effrontery to attempt to promote a pro-cartel policy by a specious appeal for free enterprise. The pretension is that freedom to compete in trade must encompass freedom to suppress competition! As though the right to start a fire in order to heat a house must include the right to burn down the house in complete disregard of the peril to the whole community! The common sense of ordinary men has no difficulty in distinguishing between the right to start a fire and the "right" to commit arson.

Unless I am greatly mistaken, the American public will no more tolerate a cartel-sanctioning abrogation of the antitrust laws in the name of "free enterprise" than they would countenance a repeal of the laws against arson in the name of "freedom of self-preservation"—the right to keep warm!

It is significant, and deserves thoughtful reflection that Germany, the "classic land of the cartel," where regimented economic restrictionism is the accepted "way of life," has in the course of two generations farrowed Kaiserism and Hitlerism—the natural offspring of militarism and cartelism. Even in times of peace, the militarists and industrial monopolists of Germany found cartel restrictions an excellent means for conducting covert warfare. In this way industrial "colonies" were acquired and prospective victims "softened up." Back in 1883, Joseph Chamberlain, as a member of the British Cabinet, declared, in sponsoring a bill designed to forefend the sub-rosa "invasion" tactics of imperialistic Germany:

"It has been pointed out especially in an interesting memorial presented on behalf of the chemical industry that under the present law it would have been possible, for instance, for the German inventor of the hot blast furnace, if he had chosen to refuse a license in England, to have destroyed almost the whole iron industry of this country and to carry the business bodily over to Germany. Although that did not happen in the case of the hot blast industry, it had actually happened in the manufacture of artificial colors connected with the coal products, and the whole of that had gone to Germany because the patentees would not grant a license in this country."

A quarter century later, Lloyd George, introducing a more drastic bill for curbing these insidious depredations on strategically vital British industries, pointed out:

"Big foreign syndicates have one very effective way of destroying British industry. They first of all apply for patents on a very considerable scale. They suggest every possible combination, for instance, in chemicals, which human ingenuity can possibly think of. These combinations the syndicates have not tried themselves. They are not in operation, say, in Germany or elsewhere. . . . A good many of these patents have been taken out not for the purpose of working the patents in this country, *but for the purpose of preventing their being worked.*"

The "big foreign syndicates" to which George referred were, of course, the German cartels.

The adroit strategy of stealthily sapping the industrial foundations of the national security of countries capable of resisting the German *drang nach* all-points-of-the-compass has been relentlessly pursued and resourcefully developed, through thick and thin, decade after decade. If the cartels are thwarted in the use of the patent system as a weapon for disarming potential competitors abroad, they may inveigle the intended victims of German aggression to a 'simulated' love-feast at which the latter are gorged with the poisoned food of production quotas, technology restrictions, market-territory limitations, and pricing inhibitions. What these tactics accomplished in the way of immobilizing French industry is now a familiar story. To cite the record of only three of the most strategic industries, through cartel manipulations the Germans succeeded in (a) reducing the relative output of French steel from substantial equality with German output in 1926 to 40 percent thereof in 1938, (b) retarding the growth of French aluminum production to a rate which fell short of doubling the output in the same period, while German production was increasing five-fold, and (c) restricting the French dyestuffs industry in such fashion that its output in 1937 was barely two-thirds of what it had been in 1924, whereas German production, even according to official estimates (none too reliable though they are) had increased five percent in the same period.

Nor were the European countries alone the "potential enemies" whose vital economic defenses were thus impaired by subtly imposed cartel restrictions. In this hemisphere, likewise and not least of all in our own country, the cartel device was sedulously—and effectively—used for the same ulterior purpose. As President Woodrow Wilson declared shortly after the first World War,

"Our complete dependence upon German [dyestuffs] supplies before the war made the interruption of trade a cause of exceptional economic disturbance. The close relation between the manufacture of dyestuffs on the one hand and of explosives and poisonous gases on the other, moreover, has given the industry an exceptional significance. . . It will . . . be a policy of obvious prudence to make certain of the successful maintenance of many strong and well-equipped chemical plants. German chemical industry, with which we will be brought into competition, was and may well be again *a thoroughly knit monopoly, capable of exercising a competition of a peculiarly insidious and dangerous kind.*"

Despite this warning in 1919, we were only slightly better off, relatively, in respect of the arts of organic chemicals manufacture twenty years later, when Germany decided the time was ripe for another attempt at world conquest, than we had been in 1917. In the matter of synthetic rubber technique, today the most strategically critical of all these processes, I. G. Farbenindustrie had succeeded, through its cartel arrangements with the leading American firms in the petroleum and chemical fields, in keeping this country in an extremely vulnerable position—as all the world now knows. Partly through persistent stalling tactics, partly through playing one American firm off against another, partly through cajolery, and partly through deliberate deceit, the German cartelists had not only stifled the development of American technology in this field, even by their "partners" on this side of the Atlantic, but had done even better, from their standpoint. They had obtained the German patent rights and the essential know-how for the most signal contributions of American technicians to the art of synthetic rubber manufacture. And, incredible though it may seem, they had obtained these advantages without divulging a single significant detail of their own carefully guarded know-how!

As the President's Office of Facts and Figures ruefully summed up the situation in 1942:

"[The enemy] has worked for many years to weaken our military potential. Through patent controls and cartel agreements he succeeded in limiting American production and export of many vital materials. He kept the prices of these materials up and the output down. He was waging war, and he did his work well, decoying important American companies into agreements, the purpose of which they did not sense."

Thus, sixty years after a member of the British Cabinet first testified to its awareness of the menace in the insidious penetration of German cartels in the international sphere, a branch of the American Executive confirms the continuing pertinence of his observations.

How, in the face of this record, in the light of this evidence of the persistence of the cartel movement and of its chronic tendency to pervert the processes of industrial production to ulterior ends leading indefeasibly to the devastation and slaughter of war can it be contended that cartels represent a promising way to order the post-war world economy? Is it not plain, rather, that "if we would guide by the light of reason," we must reaffirm our pledge of democratic equality of opportunity for all in trade and industry, and resolutely set about the task of putting our house in order in accordance with that basic principle of American life? Is it not plain, too, that monopolistic industrial control in the domestic sphere cannot be completely achieved without the uprooting of the foci of cartel infection in

German industry? Once German industry is purged of its cartel hook-ups and monopolistic animus and all non-German industry is released from the haunting fears and seductive temptations which go so far to explain these international industrial alliances, I am confident that the prospects for the restoration of genuine freedom of enterprise and healthy competitive markets will be good. While I am not sanguine of the goal being reached forthwith and easily, "at one bound" as it were, I have an abiding faith that the dynamism of economic freedom will enable us, in the end, to surmount every obstacle erected by special privilege or vested interest on the highroad to full utilization of resources. A truly great adventure is ahead.

2
Enterprise Eclipsed

It is the determination of our people not only to gain victory over the military power of aggressors, but to establish securely the lasting conditions of peace. We know that beyond victory we shall have to face a multitude of perplexing economic problems. We must also realize that we shall meet new dangers to those free institutions on which our national economy is based. If the problems of peace are to be solved, we shall have to come to grips with these difficulties in the same spirit of resolution with which the war has been waged.

It seems abundantly clear that America can never have a foreign policy based on the principles of democracy and international good will as long as international trade is dominated by cartels. It does not seem possible that the Atlantic Charter, the Good Neighbor policy, and the reciprocal trade pacts can effectively prevail if the special privileges of cartels dominate trade and politics in the postwar world.

In many respects cartels form one of the central issues of the present period. The greatest threat to our success in achieving full production and full employment at home, and friendly co-operation with other nations abroad, is the philosophy and practice of privilege embodied in cartels. If there is to be a free and productive economy in the United States, or a free exchange of goods in world markets, the power of cartels must be broken.

It is essential to understand that cartels seek to divide and rule world industry on the basis of economic privilege. If cartels are successful in gaining a foothold in the postwar period, it will be almost impossible for this nation to maintain a high level of peacetime production or to cooperate in the reconstruction of world trade.

In general, cartels restrict rather than promote trade. Cartels typically engage in such practices as dividing fields of operation and market areas between members so as to eliminate competition, restricting production by agreement, and fixing prices so as to avoid price competition. They also promote various kinds of patent licensing contracts which enable them to control and limit the use of new inventions and thus restrict the benefits of technological advance. The effects of these practices include reduced production and employment, higher prices and profits, retarded spread of technological improvements and a lower standard of living.

The conduct of cartels before and during this war has been one of the tragic pages of our history. The shortages of aluminum and magnesium resulting from cartel restrictions forced us to strip the kitchens of America and scar our public squares with scrap piles. The scarcity of rubber is a never-ceasing threat to our productive effort. Our armed forces plead with us to contribute our binoculars. The lack of vital drugs and medicines has jeopardized our men fighting in fever stricken areas. In fact, almost wherever there was a cartel there was a shortage.

But cartels have an even more serious aspect. These private governments threaten the sovereignty of democratic nations. The political implications of cartel activity threaten to subvert future national public policy of the United States.

There is a close relation between a country's economic policies and its foreign relations. It is generally recognized now that economic freedom cannot be attained at home if private groups are permitted to acquire monopoly power over industry. Likewise, it must be equally recognized that friendship and cooperation between this country and other nations cannot be established without the free exchange of goods and services. Reciprocal trade treaties and good neighbor policies can have little effect if private cartels can shut off American markets to foreign producers or prevent American producers from selling abroad.

The Good Neighbor policy is one of the fundamental principles of our relations with Latin America. While our Government was bending every effort to bring about the conditions of sound and mutually advantageous cooperation, cartels were systematically undermining these efforts. Latin America was turned over, by private cartels, as a colony to hostile foreign interests. By giving German industry virtually a free hand in Latin America, and by agreeing not to compete, American cartelists made possible the creation of a German sphere of influence. Nazi propaganda, espionage, and subversive activity all stem directly from this unhampered German penetration. When South Americans sought to purchase drugs, metals, precision equipment, and munitions from the United States, private cartel treaties had already provided that American concerns could not engage in this trade. Not only was the healthy development of South American trade and industry checked, but even today we struggle desperately to overcome the political consequences of cartel activity.

We have long cherished the principle of open covenants openly arrived at. In fact, this policy is an essential part of America's conduct of foreign affairs. Every treaty commitment made by this country is debated publicly by the people's representatives. Without the agreement of two-thirds of the Senate and the President, no treaty may be made. Yet agreements have been made in international industry affecting both the American economy and our foreign policy which were secretly contrived and clandestinely arrived at. The American people had no voice, but they bore the burden of these private treaties.

Make no mistake—the war has not interfered with cartel plans. Cartel agreements invariably provide for the contingency of war. Long before the war, cartels worked out a modus vivendi—a method of continued existence—for they felt that their relations must be preserved, war or no war. Thus we find American and British cartelists agreeing to preserve the German position in Latin American markets after the war. Agreements between the cartel members of countries now at war provide for a resumption at the war's close. In case legislation or government action interfere, then they will cooperate to adapt their relations, as one agreement states, "in the spirit of the present agreements."

Therefore, the necessity for vigorous action in keeping open the channels of trade becomes apparent when we consider that those who create cartels hold themselves above the law or seek to control legislation and Government policy in the many countries where they operate.

These same groups are making their own postwar plans. Because they have found the enforcement of the Sherman Act a hindrance in the past they have expressed a desire to have the antitrust laws repealed.

It should be recalled that the political deal which Munich represented had its economic counterpart in one made at Dusseldorf, in which the Federation of British Industries and the German industrial overlords expressed their intention of stabilizing and rationalizing world trade. As indicated at Dusseldorf, cartel groups regard governments as handy instruments to be used in working out their schemes of restriction.

Although the peace of Munich has received considerable public consideration, little attention has been given to the peace of Dusseldorf, a peace which, while obscured in the welter of political and military crises, epitomized the spirit and the power of international industrial monopoly.

On March 15 and 16, 1939, immediately after Hitler's invasion of Czechoslovakia, representatives of the Reichsgruppe Industrie of Germany and of the Federation of British Industries held an intensive conference at Dusseldorf. At the conclusion of the conference representatives of German and British industry issued the following joint declaration:

"The Reichsgruppe Industrie and the Federation of British Industries, having concluded a general discussion on Anglo-German trade relations, issue the following agreed statement:

"1. The two organizations welcome the opportunity which these discussions have given of developing still further the friendly relations which have existed between the two bodies for so many years.

. . . .

"4. The two bodies are agreed that the objective to be attained is that the export of all countries should be conducted in such a way as to ensure a fair return for the producers of those countries. Hence it is agreed that it is essential to replace destructive competition wherever it may be found by constructive cooperation, designed to foster the expansion of world trade, to the mutual benefit of Great Britain, Germany and all other countries.

"5. The two organizations are agreed that it is desirable that individual industries in both countries should endeavor to arrive at industrial agreements which will eliminate destructive competition, wherever occurring, but prices must be fixed at such a level as not to diminish the buying power of the consumers.

"6. The two organizations realize that agreements upon prices or other factors between Germany and Great Britain are only a step, although a most important step, towards a more ordered system of world trade. They would welcome the participation of other nations in such agreements.

. . . .

"8. The two organizations realize that in certain cases the advantages of agreements between the industries of two countries or of a group of countries may be nullified by competition from the industry in some other country that refuses to become a party to the agreement. In such circumstances it may be necessary for the organizations to obtain the help of their governments and the two organizations agree to collaborate in seeking that help.

"9. The two organizations agree that it is their objective to ensure that as a result of an agreement between their industries unhealthy competition shall be removed. Their aim is to secure as complete cooperation as possible throughout the industrial structure of their respective countries.

"10. The two organizations have agreed to use their best endeavors to promote and foster negotiations between the individual industries in their respective countries. They are encouraged in this task owing to the fact that a considerable number of agreements between individual German and British industrial groups are already in existence. There is thus available a large body of experience which inspires confidence that an immediate extension of this policy is both practicable and advantageous.

"They are glad to state that approximately a further fifty industrial groups have already signified their willingness in principle to negotiate at an early date.

"They also report with satisfaction that negotiations have already been started and are now taking place between ten industrial groups."

The spirit exemplified in the above declaration is not dead. It is awaiting the moment of peace to step in and resume control of those very industries which are most essential to the rehabilitation of a war-torn world, to the fullest use of our labor and resources.

Surely we must realize now that if the program of Dusseldorf prevails in the postwar world it will produce World War III. Surely we must recognize that we cannot build a free world without a free economy.

The close and constant cooperation of the United Nations after the war is all-important. This cooperation should rest, among other things, on active and healthy international trade. We want to see that trade grow unhampered by private restrictions. In attacking these illegal activities the Government of the United States is aiming at a condition which obstructs healthy international trade and threatens the effectiveness of governmental foreign policies.

To combat the influence of monopoly groups, the United States has two effective weapons: (1) the vigorous enforcement of the Sherman Act, and (2) the power which Congress possesses to investigate and make public the hidden dealings of cartel interests.

It is significant that in Great Britain increasing interest in the purposes and activities of cartels is being manifested—principally as the result of American antitrust investigations which have revealed that British industry, no less than our own industry, has suffered the burden of restrictive practices imposed by cartel arrangements.

Moreover, there has been developing in Canada a substantial

interest in the cartel problem. Thus, the *Ottawa Journal* recently stated editorially that "it is fairly clear to all that cartels, large combinations of industries parcelling out territories among themselves, controlling patents and fixing prices, may be a menace to the general well-being, and what is more vital, a menace to world peace."

And the *Winnipeg Free Press* declared not long ago that "it is gradually dawning upon Britain that rationalization of industry has its dangers. They are discovering that monopolies can and do develop evil practices. . . . Thus there is arising there [in Great Britain] a demand for control of monopolies, the breaking down of cartels and the restoration of competition between the great industrial giants." After pointing out some of the evils that flow from monopoly control, the *Winnipeg Free Press* went on to say: "National monopolies which restrain trade are bad enough of themselves. But when combined with international cartels they are intolerable. The Canadian government should pay particular attention to the antitrust proceedings in the United States. They reveal a most unhealthy state of industrial health and if the economy of this country is to be saved from disaster steps will have to be taken to break up the evil monopolies and their cartels."

It would certainly be in the mutual interest of Great Britain and ourselves if we could take a joint stand against private restrictive arrangements in the postwar world and together seek to stamp them out.

There is ample reason to believe that American exposure of secret cartel practices may have its effect on the public policy of other countries and promote common understanding that certain types of activity should be outlawed in other countries as well as here. But irrespective of the extent to which other governments adopt policies similar to ours, there can be no doubt that American business can thrive in competition with foreign cartels if it does not enter into cartel restrictions. If freed of cartel shackles, American enterprise should well be able to expand in world markets and render foreign cartel control ineffective. It is doubtful, indeed, whether any major international cartel can effectively control world markets without the participation and cooperation of the American segments of the industry. There is a real question whether foreign cartels can long survive in many industries if American cooperation is not extended to them.

If and when some measure of control and regulation becomes economically necessary on an international scale in a particular industry, a question is presented for governmental action—not for private cartel action. If, for example, in a particular industry it seems necessary to control production in order to avoid waste of a scarce natural resource, the solution of such a problem is properly a responsibility of national or international governmental action. Where control is needed, it must be by public authority. If international restrictive agreements are ever needed, they must be determined upon by governments—not by private cartels.

But the situation where control would be required on an international scale is decidedly the exception. Most foreign trade in the postwar world can be conducted on a competitive basis if we give competition a chance. The period following the war will present an unprecedented challenge to the ingenuity of mankind. Men of brains and imagination should have a chance to rebuild the world, to take risks, to engage in foreign trade and to win in competitive struggle, unhampered by private decrees. The world is not a private hunting preserve which can be divided at will among monopolists who think they have gained squatters' rights.

3

Technology

In the days of Adam Smith it was possible to measure the wealth of nations in terms of mineral resources, possession of fertile lands and control of strategic geographical areas. Today we have a new index to the wealth and security of nations. Technology and applied science have become principal instruments in the maintenance of a high standard of living and for the protection of national interests. In fact, when we speak of the balance of power in the modern world, we must take into account the extent and quality of industrial and technological resources as dominant factors in national welfare. The horizons which have been opened by applied science and research offer to the world, and to our own nation in particular, new industries, greater opportunities for our youth, higher levels of health and comfort, and the attainment of that genuine social security which comes with all great advancements in human knowledge.

Technology—its direction, its applications, and its enjoyment—is today a primary concern of government. In a system based upon freedom of enterprise, access to technology is the fundamental condition of rapid advancement toward the goals for which our nation is striving. The power that goes with the development of modern technology has been perverted in totalitarian countries to provide instruments of aggression. Because totalitarian states have regimented science and have made it subservient to imperial ambitions, it has been used to destroy rather than to create. One of the principal problems which the United Nations will encounter in the peace to come will be the prevention of any abuse of new discoveries for the purpose of establishing war machines which can threaten the peace of the world.

The control of vital areas of research by monopolistic interests is a condition which cannot be tolerated Monopoly control seeks to protect vested interests and to perpetuate its grip on the advancement of science and technology. It retards the introduction of new goods and services and the maintenance of full employment in time of peace. Our experiences in this war have demonstrated conclusively that monopolistic control of critical sectors of industrial research has a paralyzing effect on mobilization of our national strength. One of the most difficult problems we have encountered in arming this country has been the domination and restriction of technology by small privileged groups. It has required strenuous efforts on the part of government and industry alike to overcome the stifling effects of complacent monopoly.

With rare exceptions industrial research at the present time can only be carried on by large numbers of scientists and technicians combining their ingenuity to resolve the complex problems of both pure and applied science. In the last fifty years technology has moved at such a rapid pace that no longer is the small businessman in a position to maintain laboratories of sufficient size. Today we witness the gigantic research organizations of all major corporations, and no one desires to impair their efficiency.

There is, nevertheless, a gap between the promise of organized research conducted on a huge scale by great corporations and the fulfillment as measured by accomplishments in the public interest. So that there shall be no misunderstanding, I should like to pay tribute to the vast army of scientists and research workers who have done such remarkable work in the years of peace as well as in the years of war in bringing forth a multitude of amazing discoveries. It is not their fault that their contributions have not been fully realized. The trouble is that in many instances the misuse of research by monopolistic and cartelized groups has resulted in the restricting of production, withholding new products, and fencing in and blocking off new developments.

One of the ablest and clearest statements of the effect of restrictive arrangements upon research was made by Dr. F. B. Jewett, vice-president of the American Telephone & Telegraph, and chief of Bell Laboratories. In discussing an agreement between his company and other parties, he stated:

"Broadly speaking, the practical effect of the agreement is to limit the field of possible development of each party to its present major activities. . . .

"Thus, while a casual reading of the agreement by one not thoroughly conversant with all the factors may appear to establish the basis for an enlarged free development in most of the fields, this is not actually the case.

. . . .

"The far-reaching effect of the proposed agreement on the character and scope of our research and development work is apparent. Viewed both from the standpoint of the research worker in our laboratories and from the standpoint of those responsible for the expenditures incurred by the Laboratories, the inevitable result would be a narrowing of the field of activity and failure to undertake anything which at the outset is not clearly directed to the field of our current business. From the standpoint of the man who has a brilliant idea which in its first nebulous form seems to be applicable outside our business, there will be little or no urge to go ahead in the face of a situation where he knows that the results of his work have been sold in advance outside of the Bell System. From the standpoint of management there will likewise be no incentive, but quite the reverse, to urging him on and appropriating money for his investigations."

A member of a monopoly or cartel group all too often finds itself in a position where it must choose between the national interest on the one hand and its cartel obligations on the other. This difficulty is accurately stated in a document taken from the Standard Oil Co. (N. J.) files with reference to the development of 100 octane gasoline, one of the most vital materials of modern warfare:

"This possibility is, of course, extremely attractive to the Army Air Corps, but there is one difficulty involved which Mr. Russell quite frankly discussed. The hydrogenation development originated in Germany, and through cooperation all around has now passed into the hands of the oil industry of the entire world, and, to a certain extent, into the hands of the foreign chemical industry as well. There is a full and free exchange of technical information between all of the companies and units involved in the hydrogenation development and this exchange is not only by means of reports but by constant visits of technical men. To cut off these reports and shut our hydrogenation plants against these visitors would be not only a violation of these agreements, which would involve us in many difficulties, but would also be tantamount to a confession that we were engaged in some work of special military value which would mean that the plants would become a focal point for espionage. The costs and difficulties of protecting against leakage of information about large commercial operations under such conditions is hard to estimate. *It seems that the only practical way to handle this problem is to avoid carrying out the operation of producing* 100 *octane number aviation gasoline commercially as long as possible.* We would, of course, also have to breach our agreements to render full and complete technical reports to all of the companies associated with us (even to the American companies, for fear of leakage). We should also forfeit the advantage in producing at the least cost the best available gasoline for commercial purposes.

"*Any program by which the Army Air Corps can obtain their objective of a one or two year start over the rest of the world on this vital matter bristles with difficulties and sacrifices from our standpoint.* We will not have to cross the bridge finally until our present experiments are completed. When and if we are able to demonstrate that the hydrogenation plants are capable of turning out an aviation product which with the usual quantity of lead can be brought up to 100 octane number, we shall be faced with the situation mentioned above. *To meet the very proper desires of the Air Corps as expressed to us we shall have to violate our agreements and perhaps forfeit the confidence of our associates, both American and foreign, and beyond this we shall either have to avoid any commercial use of the new method or run the very grave risk of finding that our efforts at secrecy have been abortive.*"

In pointing out the inevitable conflicts between national loyalties and business interests which arise when industry is carried on through private international cartel agreements, I do not attack, nor do I intend to cast aspersions against, the patriotic motives of any men or companies. I assume that the persons who have taken part in these transactions have not consciously acted against the best interests of their country. But it is the cartel system that is at fault. The individuals caught up in the system are faced with a dilemma because it imposes on them choices which it is almost impossible to make without violation of an obligation to one of two conflicting interests.

One of the most serious limitations upon research has been the division of fields of technology by cartel groups. If a company is barred by agreement from an aspect of technology, there is little if any incentive to do research in that field. One possible consequence of such division of technology is that it permits foreign interests to exercise influence amounting to domination over research in this country.

No one doubts that synthetic rubber is a matter of national interest. The cartel arrangement between Standard Oil Co. (N. J.) and I. G. Farbenindustrie was such that the latter dominated the development of synthetic rubber in this country as well as in Germany.

In the case of the Bausch & Lomb (Rochester)-Carl Zeiss (Jena, Germany) cartel on military optical glass, the heads of the Bausch & Lomb department responsible for military research were to be appointed only with the agreement of the Zeiss firm.

In regard to the cartel involving Plexiglass, probably one of the most important plastics, and one which has innumerable military uses, the Rohm & Haas Company (Philadelphia) stated: "We could think of a price agreement on the finished product, or a division of our interests . . . we have not only our own interests at stake, but also the ones of our German house [Rohm & Haas of Darmstadt, Germany] and the I. G."

In December 1934 a high official of the duPont Company wrote to E. W. Webb, president of the Ethyl Gasoline Corporation (copies were sent to every member of its Board of Directors) as follows:

"I learned through our Organic Chemicals Division today that the Ethyl Gasoline Corporation has in mind forming a German company with the I. G. to manufacture Ethyl lead in that country.

"I have just had two weeks in Washington, no inconsiderable part of which was devoted to criticising the interchanging with foreign companies of chemical knowledge which might have a military value. Such giving of information by an industrial company might have the gravest repercussions on it. The Ethyl Gasoline Corporation would be no exception, in fact, would probably be singled out for special attack because of the ownership of its stock.

"It would seem, on the face of it, that the quantity of Ethyl lead used for commercial purposes in Germany would be too small to go after. It has been claimed that Germany is secretly arming. Ethyl lead would doubtless be a valuable aid to military aeroplanes.

"I am writing you this to say that in my opinion under no conditions should you or the Board of Directors of the Ethyl Gasoline Corporation disclose any secrets or 'know how' in connection with the manufacture of tetra-ethyl lead to Germany."

Yet, in the face of this warning from duPont, on January 12, 1935, Webb wrote the Chief of the Army Air Corps that "There is no technical data of military importance known to us which would be involved in the building of such a plant that has not already received wide publicity, or is of common knowledge in the aviation field."

This statement strikingly ignores the warning received from duPont only one month earlier that such a disclosure would "doubtless" be prejudicial to our national security. In this connection it should not be overlooked that duPont and Dow were the sole producers of the chemical components of tetraethyl lead and, as such, were the concerns which alone possessed the essential know-how.

Why did Ethyl Gasoline disregard duPont's warning? Webb himself has supplied the answer in the final paragraph of his letter of January 12, 1935:

"There is, furthermore, an equally, if not more, important business aspect to the German situation. We are owned by Standard Oil and General Motors in equal shares. General Motors has important investments in Germany, producing there in excess of 50 percent of the motor cars. Standard Oil has large investments in all phases of the petroleum business in Germany. . . . We feel . . . for the reasons specifically mentioned here, that it would be extremely unfortunate for all concerned if we do not proceed to carry out the agreement with I. G. . . . A refusal or undue delay on our part . . . might bring on some serious reprisal measures."

This leaves nothing for surmise. It is not unfair to conclude, in view of these facts, that for the directors of Ethyl Gasoline the preservation of I. G. good-will conflicted with the maintenance of good faith in dealings with their own government. Though duPont, from the beginning, was opposed to the entire deal on grounds of patriotic scruples, nevertheless it eventually deferred. In an inter-office memo of the duPont Company appears the following:

"I think we should tell I.C.I. that the technical and engineering information which we are giving I. G. in connection with Tetraethyl Lead is being given them entirely at the request of the Ethyl Gasoline Corporation. As they no doubt know, Ethyl Gas and I. G. set up some arrangements whereby they are going to participate jointly in the manufacture and sale of Ethyl Lead in Germany and we are turning over our information to Ethyl Gas which they in turn can submit to I. G. as part of the bargain in connection with this joint enterprise."

The full extent of the dilemma in which cartel members are placed by the conflict of their cartel commitments with national interest is indicated in two statements made by a representative of one of the world's great industrial combines. In a letter written in 1939, after the outbreak of war, a Standard Oil official stated:

"Pursuant to these arrangements I was able to keep my appointments in Holland, where I had three days of discussion with the representatives of the I. G. They delivered to me assignments of some 2,000 foreign patents and *we did our best to work out complete plans for a modus vivendi which would operate through the term of the war, whether or not the U. S. came in.* All of the arrangements could not be completed, but it is hoped that enough has been done to permit closing the most important uncompleted points by cable. It is difficult to visualize as yet just how successful we shall be in maintaining our relations through this period without personal contacts."

It is of significance also that this same representative of a cartel group brilliantly expressed the cartel point of view when he said:

"Upon completion of that agreement, the war intervened because our grouping of interested parties included Americans, British, Dutch, Germans, and the war introduced quite a number of complications. *How we are going to make these belligerent parties lie down in the same bed isn't quite clear as yet.* We are now addressing ourselves to that phase of the problem and I hope we will find some solution. *Technology has to carry on*

—*war or no war*—so we must find some solution to these last problems."

It is in their very nature that cartels restrict the fullest developments of new products and that they attempt to place rigid handicaps on output. Very often they even adulterate the quality of products in order to exact the greatest possible toll from the public. Several examples may be used to indicate the practices and mental attitude of monopoly groups in relation to the quality of material. The following quotation concerning flashlight bulbs speaks for itself:

"Two or three years ago we proposed a reduction in the life of flashlight lamps from the old basis on which one lamp was supposed to outlast three batteries, to a point where the life of the lamp and the life of the battery under service conditions would be approximately equal. Sometime ago, the battery manufacturers went part way with us on this and accepted lamps of two battery lives instead of three. This has worked out very satisfactorily.

"We have been continuing our studies and efforts to bring about the use of one battery life lamps. I think you will be interested in the attached analysis which Messrs. Prideaux and Egeler have worked up covering the various points involved in going to the one battery life basis. If this were done, we estimate that it would result in increasing our flashlight business approximately 60 per cent. We can see no logical reason either from our standpoint or that of the battery manufacturer why such a change should not be made at this time.

"Messrs. Parker and Johnson now have this matter up with the battery manufacturers and I would urge that every assistance be given them to put it over."

Methyl methacrylate, the name of one of the best known plastics, is used not only in the industrial field to make airplane windshielding and many other structural materials, but it also has excellent qualities for the making of dental plates or dentures. As a result of the monopoly control of this material by the duPont Company and Rohm & Haas, its uses were divided into two fields: industrial and dental. At the time these firms were indicted a sharp difference in price was maintained. When methyl methacrylate was sold for industrial purposes, it cost 85 cents a pound, while the price to dental users was $45 a pound. The dental profession soon learned that there was no difference in the material, whether it was designed for industrial or dental use. As a result they began to purchase their requirements from industrial users, in order to gain the advantage of the cheaper industrial price which, we could assume, might possibly be passed on to the dental patient.

The monopoly clique considered this a form of bootlegging. On March 15, 1940, the Vernon-Benshoff Company (Pittsburgh), a member of the clique, made various suggestions to the Rohm and Haas Company which, although they were not placed in actual effect, offer valuable insight into the shocking extremes to which monopolists will consider going:

"Our discussion of the Pure Food and Drug Law and pulling the acrylic denture under it leads me to wonder if the manufacturers of the commercial molding powders might not add an ingredient which would not effect the molding properties, but which would disqualify it under the act. Apparently a slight trace would suffice. Naturally it would be omitted from the strictly denture powder.

"Recently I asked Dr. Johnson to suggest an addition which might interfere with distillation of monomer or retard polymerization. He could not think of anything that wouldn't spoil the molding properties or clarity of the powders. But there the quantity needed to accomplish the result was the handicap.

"Under the very finicky regulations of the above act however, it may be the slightest trace of the right agent, too little to constitute harm to molding (or health either as a matter of fact) would suffice to have bootleg products in bad.

"A millionth of one per cent of arsenic or lead might cause them to confiscate every bootleg unit in the country. There ought to be a trace of something that would make them rear up."

In its reply the Rohm & Haas Company said that it was in agreement with the general principles presented in the letter quoted above and that it would ask its research department to work on the matter. This was expressed in a letter of March 21, 1940 to the Vernon-Benshoff firm:

"With reference to your letter of March 15th, we shall be glad to investigate whether denture materials come under the Pure Food and Drug Act. We agree with you that if we could put some ingredient in our commercial molding material which would disqualify it under the Pure Food and Drug Act, this would be a very fine method of controlling the bootleg situation. We shall take this matter up with our development department and advise you whether any such material could be used."

A striking way in which research can be perverted is illustrated by another example. The dyestuffs industry is one which is basically monopolistic and cartelized. A tight grip is maintained over its price structure. This is especially true of dyestuffs for textiles. Recently the duPont Company's research laboratories developed a pigment which can be utilized either in paints or as a dye for textiles. The duPont research laboratories considered various ways to be sure that the pigment could be limited in use to the paint and finishing field so as not to disturb the price structure of the textile dyestuffs field. The trend of duPont's research thought on this subject was stated by the director of one of its laboratories:

"Further work may be necessary on adding contaminants to 'Monastral' colors to make them unsatisfactory on textiles but satisfactory for paints."

After working on this problem for some time, duPont's Jackson Laboratory reported on its progress somewhat dolefully. (DuPont says of Jackson Laboratory that it is "one of the largest organic chemical research laboratories in the world.") The particular task involved was difficult, according to a report by the Jackson Laboratory dated June 26, 1940:

"Mr. Chantler was of the opinion that pigment mixtures, unsuitable for textile printing would be very difficult to obtain.

"(B) *Agents Injurious to Textile Printing.*—The suggestion was made that certain compounds that were white under ordinary conditions but that would be oxidized to give colored bodies when the prints are subjected to chlorine bleach, could be used. A few experiments had been made along this line using such compounds as Chlorostain N, dianisidine and DuPont Oxy Black Base. Complete data on this work are not available. Mr. Dahlen expressed the opinion that the addition of such compounds probably would cause as much or more damage to the paint trade as to textile printing.

"Such substances as ground glass and carborundum were suggested for incorporation with the pigment. While these materials would undoubtedly scratch printing rolls, there is considerable doubt as to their effect in paints and lacquers."

Two days later the problem was again attacked at a meeting between the representatives of General Aniline Works and the duPont Company. Eight possible methods of adulteration were considered. I quote a few from the confidential memorandum of their discussion:

"1. A new type of copper phthalocyanine (CPC) for the paint and lacquer trade which would be unsuitable for application textiles.

. . . .

"The importance of solving these problems was recognized, and it was agreed that both parties would work on promising ideas which resulted from this discussion. The three problems are closely related, and it is possible that the solution of one or two will automatically solve the third. It was agreed that a powder would be the preferable standard. After detailed discussion of various modes of attack, the following appeared to be outstanding:

"1. (a) Mixtures of CPC with Lakes.—The most promising mode of attack appears to lie in the formulation of a mixture of CPC with a lake, especially a lake of CPC. Such a mixture should have fairly good fastness to light and *yet be poor in wash fastness on textiles* or incompatible with the usual textile printing lacquers . . .

. . . .

"(d) Deteriorate Cotton.—Compounds might be incorporated into CPC which when applied to textiles and followed by bleaching or heating treatment *might increase the deterioration of the cloth.* Compounds such as chlorates or aliphatic halides which would produce hydrochloric acid were specific examples.

. . . .

"(g) Irritating Substances.—*It is known that certain resins and solvents are irritating to the skin, often causing dermatitis. It might be possible to formulate a CPC composition which will make textile materials irritating to the skin.*

"(h) Incorporation of Grit.—It seemed too dangerous to attempt to add gritty material to CPC since, although it would interfere with the use of the material for textiles, it would also offer serious disadvantages in grinding on application of surface coatings.

"It was agreed that the mere dulling of the material would not be a satisfactory solution since dull shades are often used in the textile trade. Most of the above comments are often based on work on blue, and many of the solutions would apply equally well to the green. In fact it is believed that there is a larger market for the sale of green than the blue."

It seems to me that we cannot afford to place our sole reliance upon monopolistic corporations whose interests have only too often been divided, who have sought restricted production rather than full employment of our resources and labor, and who have sought for monopoly control rather than public welfare. We must learn by the bitter lessons of the early years of this war which found us lacking both materials and the know-how to make them, resulting from the restrictive practices of monopolies which instinctively seek to produce as little as possible for the greatest profit.

In war and peace alike technology is a vital factor in our national life. The present war is being waged with weapons and equipment which represent the last word in scientific development. Careful planning and rigorous adherence to the plans enabled Germany to have, in 1939, the most efficient war machine the world had ever seen. Now, after several years of feverish activity, the United Nations have at last caught up with and passed Germany in the race for armament superiority.

Now that our war effort has finally been put in high gear an entirely different kind of problem seems to be emerging. Under the forced draft of war urgency and unlimited government expenditure, materials and products are being made the like of which we have not heretofore known. The light metals, aluminum and magnesium, the wonder metal beryllium, the miraculously efficient diamond tools and the tungsten carbide tools, the plastics and dozens of other new developments will unquestionably make the postwar world something entirely different from that to which we have been accustomed. Many of the processes which can revolutionize our mode of living are owned by the government. Some are in the custody of the Alien Property Custodian. Others have been developed with federal funds, either by government agencies or by private concerns. No one will seriously dispute the wisdom of retaining control of these government-owned processes and of fostering the fullest possible use of them for the benefit of all.

There can be no denying that the war has resulted in a concentration of productive facilities in the hands of a relatively small number of gigantic corporations. Even before Pearl Harbor some of them were enormous concerns capable of wielding irresistible power in the competitive struggle with other, smaller companies. Today and after the war the smaller competitors which have survived will find the odds against them a great deal more disheartening than before. It is not in the public interest to allow the small competitors to be killed off in the uneven fight. Neither is it in the public interest to place hampering restrictions upon the efforts of the large companies to fully utilize their research laboratories and technical experience for the purpose of strengthening their competitive position.

Without doubt the sensible thing for us to do is to make research and technology available to the little fellow as well as to his big competitor. In agriculture this policy has amply demonstrated its soundness. Experiment stations financed by state and federal funds extend the benefits of their research to the small farmer as well as to the large. It is doubtful that one could find a single intelligent farm operator, large or small, who would voice the opinion that governmentally financed agricultural research has not been worth many times the money spent for it. The small industrialist has the same right to expect that a government wishing him to continue to make his contribution to the national welfare shall offer him those benefits of research and expert advice which he cannot afford to provide for himself but which can easily be provided by the government.

There are those who scoff at all mention of cartels and refer to them as bogies conjured up to justify an attack on all big business. Such an attitude is dangerous. Cartels present the greatest challenge to our system of free enterprise.

In every cartel arrangement which has come to the attention of the Antitrust Division of the Department of Justice technology has been a vital factor. It is the responsibility of government to see that technology remains free from artificial control and monopoly perversion.

Every instance of this sort is evidence of the possibility of service to the public which might be expected if the government should see fit to provide itself with an adequately financed and numerically sufficient staff of technologists. It is my belief that the time has arrived for the adoption of legislation which will adequately protect and advance the public interest in technological development.

4

Patents

The importance and the position of patents in the American economy have been sharply defined since the outbreak of the present war. While the problem which patents have presented to our economy did not begin with the attack on Pearl Harbor, our experience within the past few years has crystallized many of the questions and issues at stake.

Patents are fundamental factors in the cartel problem because patent agreements are quite frequently used as the basis of cartel arrangements. The vital importance of control over technology and research to the achievement of cartel power enhances the significance of patents as the foundation stones of cartel structures. At the same time, the effects of patent abuses upon the economy are magnified to a critical degree.

We are all familiar with the historical background of the patent system and with the intent of the authors of the Constitution in stating that Congress shall have the power to promote the progress of science and useful arts by the grant of a patent. It is no accident that the original clause in the Constitution was phrased in careful terms. The framers of the Constitution inherited a concern toward the grant of any monopoly by government. They were specific in limiting the scope of the patent monopoly because they did not wish the patent to become the basis of a system of privilege.

When the American patent system was born, we were a frontier nation. Pioneers in every branch of science had before them an inviting horizon of discovery. The recognition of their contribution towards the promotion of science and useful arts served as a stimulus to their initiative and ingenuity. During this period the patent system served our country well and acted as a major incentive in the making of industrial America.

Our patent system was designed to "promote the progress of science and useful arts." In many respects it has done so, and has given proper protection to inventors and enterprising businessmen. Where it operates to carry out this purpose, there can be no just complaint. But in many instances the patent system has been perverted to accomplish exactly the opposite effect. The patent has become the principal power weapon of modern monopoly, and the misuse of patents the major tactic of industrial cartels. This perversion has become so widespread as to jeopardize the whole patent system.

The patent problem as it exists today arises in an environment vastly different from the handicraft era in which modern industry found its beginnings. It is not the patent grant as such nor is it the operation of the individual inventor that brings the patent system into question. Invention today is a large-scale industry in a complex economy. In many branches of industrial production vast monopolies exercise a dominating influence over research. It is the abuse and misuse of patents by such concentrated groups wielding tremendous economic power which have brought patents into conflict with the fundamental purpose of the patent law and with the Sherman Act.

Monopoly interests which have violated the antitrust laws in the course of their abuse of patents have made the claim that the Antitrust Division of the Department of Justice is endangering the patent system by prosecuting restraints of trade based on patents. Many honest and innocent bystanders have been confused and misled by this propaganda. The fact of the matter is that danger to the patent system arises not from enforcement of the antitrust laws but from the flagrant abuses of those who use patents as the foundation stone of illegal monopolistic control of industry. If the patent system is finally wrecked we shall have to thank those who brought it into disrepute by their unflagging attempts to use the patent grant in a manner contrary both to the law and to the national interest.

Because patents have become an instrument of power-hungry and power-seeking groups in industry, grave doubt now exists as to whether our economy can longer tolerate and permit the control and consolidation of patents by industrial oligarchies.

Among the many serious abuses to which patents have become subject within the last few decades, it is necessary to specify only a few.

1. Patents have been used illegally to establish regimented systems of industrial control by private groups.

2. Patents have been used, contrary to the tradition and intent of the American economy, to stifle new enterprise, to limit capacity and production, to divide world markets, to impose artificial and arbitrary price levels, and to set up private tariff walls.

3. In their determination to eliminate competition among themselves and to prevent the emergence of new enterprise, monopoly groups in industry have used patents as a shield for conspiracy to violate the antitrust laws.

4. Employing the instruments of law designed to secure justice and protection to the small inventor and small business-

man, monopoly interests have used litigation and threats of litigation based on patents to compel the submission or surrender of independent enterprise to the dictates of monopoly control.

5. Patents have been used by industrial giants here and abroad to fasten their grip on international trade by setting up patent cartel agreements which slice world markets into exclusive trade areas. In many instances these international patent cartels have made it plain that they consider adherence to monopoly rules to be above and beyond the laws of the United States and other countries.

6. Our experiences in the first World War and the present global war have demonstrated conclusively that the interests of hostile countries have been able to use patents as weapons in economic warfare against the United States. By delaying the development of strategic new industries, by withholding know-how, and by strangling the market with exorbitant prices for critical materials, monopoly groups in aggressor nations have sought to weaken the war potential of the American economy.

7. In numerous instances, scientific research has been perverted and misused in order to strengthen monopoly restrictions illegally based on patents.

In the scores of Department of Justice cases involving patents and illegal agreements based on patents and in the testimony before various congressional committees investigating the facts, it has become overwhelmingly clear that if free enterprise is to be maintained, patent abuses must be eliminated. At the same time, the protection which the patent right was designed to give to the independent inventor and businessman must be strengthened and restored. If the system of economic competition on which this nation depends for its well-being is to be preserved, it is imperative that economic opportunity be granted to all on equal terms. This cannot be accomplished if privileged groups are able to obtain unfair advantage over new enterprise or to amass huge patent structures which block the road to industrial initiative.

In a whole roster of industries, patents have been employed as the police power of private economic governments. Our industrial history is replete with examples of industries dominated by a few small monopoly groups whose power rested on patents. In the radio industry, in explosives, in spectacles, in glass containers, in magnesium, in vitamins, in medicines, in building materials, in dyestuffs, in electrical equipment and in synthetic rubber, to mention prominent examples, the development of the industry has been decided by the arbitrary discretion of groups controlling concentrated patent structures. Using patents as an excuse, monopolists have sought to determine who shall be given permission to manufacture, to buy and to sell. They have determined what prices should be fixed and in what markets sales might be made. In illegally wielding their patent power such groups have completely squelched free enterprise in these and in many other industries. Such control is regimentation and bureaucracy in an extreme and pernicious form. The independent businessman who falls victim to this system of control is without recourse.

Many businessmen seriously object to the regulation of industry by government. What they do not realize is that it is not public government but private government which exercises the most rigid control over industrial conduct. Such regimentation violates the fundamental and elementary principles of economic liberty. If we believe in free enterprise we cannot at the same time tolerate the existence of private economic government which bears no responsibility to the public. This type of regimentation has acquired such influence in numerous branches of industry that free enterprise no longer operates.

A striking example of the manner in which patents are misused to create private industrial governments is afforded by the glass container industry. For more than a generation this industry has been dominated by a monopoly group whose main function it has been to acquire and license patents. This private governing body produced nothing itself, yet the production of practically all the glass containers made in this country was subject to its will. The amount of glass containers to be produced by any manufacturer was closely regulated and limited. The type of bottle he could make was determined by a system which permitted practically no competition. Outsiders who attempted to enter the industry were promptly eliminated by vigorous and costly patent suits.

The patent policy of the monopoly group was neatly set forth in a company memorandum which states:

"In taking out patents we have three main purposes: (a) To cover the actual machines which we are putting out and prevent duplication of them . . . (b) to block the development of machines which might be constructed by others for the same purpose as our machines, using alternative means; (c) to secure patents on possible improvements of competing machines so as to 'fence in' those and prevent their reaching an improved stage . . ."

In the administration and regulation of the glass container industry, this group pursued a licensing policy equally intended to perpetuate its monopolistic position. In a memorandum outlining this aspect of its control, the following statement appears:

"Consequently, we adopted the policy which we have followed ever since, of restricted licensing. That is to say, (a) We licensed the machines only to selected manufacturers of the better type, refusing many licenses whom we thought would be price cutters, and (b) We restricted their fields of manufacture, in each case, to certain specific articles, with the idea of preventing too much competition. (c) In order to retain more complete control of th situation, we retained title to the machines and simply leased them for a definite period of years, usually 8 or 10 years, with the privilege of renewal of a smaller additional term."

Obviously, the patent and licensing policy in the glass container industry constitutes a system of oppressive regulation which neither promotes the progress of science and the useful arts nor permits the operation of competitive economic processes. Yet, instances like the glass container industry could be multiplied for it is by no means unique in modern American industry.

The restrictive effects of patent abuses on the production of critical materials in this country became clearly apparent following the outbreak of war. Shortage followed shortage, and in nearly every instance the basic device restricting our expansion of capacity and output was found to be a patent cartel agreement.

A dramatic illustration of a shortage resulting from a restrictive patent agreement enforced by cartel groups is provided in the case of tungsten carbide. Few items are as important as machine tools to our economy both in peace and in war. The best cutting edge for machine tools is made from tungsten carbide. Because of a patent cartel agreement between the General Electric Company of this country and the Krupp Works of Germany, the price was maintained at such a high level that the second largest manufacturer of this commodity said:

"The control of the tungsten carbide patents by the General Electric Company and the Krupp Company has resulted in keeping the prices at exorbitant levels. Now when the emergency has come, industry has not learned how to use tungsten carbide and has not the machines, the skilled men, or the technique which it would have had if the material had been available at the same low prices at which it was available to German industries."

Before the patent cartel was organized, the price in the United States was less than $50 a pound. After the cartel was formed in 1928, the price of tungsten carbide rose to as high as $453 a pound or, in other words, much more than the price of gold. Significantly enough, the price in Germany never rose above $50 a pound.

While we recognize that technology is the most dynamic factor of change in the modern world, it is not sufficiently realized that in the struggle to control technological development and to confine research within their feudal domains, monopolistic interests divide the universe of technology in exactly the same way that they parcel out world territory. Using the huge patent structures which they have erected, industrial giants divide among themselves the major branches of technology and allow no one to encroach on their preserves.

Although we depend upon research as the principal source of those advances which promise a better and a healthier world, we tend to overlook the fact that the power which modern monopoly wields over research, by virtue of patents, often perverts the spirit of discovery. How the deliberate misdirection of research is carried out is clearly indicated in at least three cases involving electric lamps, plastics, and dyestuffs.

Electric lamps in the United States are practically the private preserve of a domestic monopoly. The history of this industry can be written in terms of the elimination of competition, based largely on the abuse of patent litigation and price fixing. One of the great threats to monopoly control can come from the virility and imagination of our inventive genius. For this reason the vested interests attempt not only to control their current monopoly, but take every precaution to project their control into the future and to guard against the development and exploitation of inventions by outsiders.

One of the greatest developments in the lighting art since Edison invented the incandescent lamp is fluorescent lighting. It has already proven to be many times more efficient, and cheaper, than incandescent lighting. The rapid development of this newer type of lighting which would come from a competitive situation has been carefully suppressed by the monopoly group. Patent control by the monopoly group controlling incandescent lamps has been the main instrument for the suppression of fluorescent lighting. Not only the monopoly group governing incandescent lighting, but the electric utility companies as well, fear the effects of the widespread use of more efficient means of lighting, since it would reduce their sale of electricity and hence their profits. A letter from the manager of the lighting bureau of a large power company to the General Electric Company should be of interest to the public:

"Increasingly I seem to become the 'father confessor' on fluorescent lighting as far as the utility men are concerned. This concerns one of the displays dealing with fluorescent lighting in your G. E. building at the New York World's Fair. I must confess that although I have been in your exhibit twice I did not see this particular display.

"It appears that 20 watts of fluorescent lighting are compared with 20 watts of incandescent lighting, the sign purporting to read something to the effect 'See the difference between equal wattages of fluorescent and mazda lighting.' Of course, the readings on the foot candle meters show dramatic differences.

"If this demonstration is as explained to us, I think it does *violate the spirit of the understanding that our group had in*

Cleveland. As a matter of fact, I would think it violated the fundamental concept of the lamp department that advances in the lighting art should not be at the expense of wattage, but should give the customer more for the same money. I hope you can find a way to change this exhibit, so that it does not give misleading impressions to the crowd who will see it."

Here is the reply by the General Electric Company:

"When Miss Winters showed me the attached letter . . . I immediately got in touch with Al Reas with regard to the demonstration at the fair. Apparently this particular demonstration was temporarily loaned for use at the fair, and is now being returned to the exhibit shop. *Therefore, by removing this particular exhibit, Sharp and the other utility men need have nothing to worry about.*"

Even if such flagrant misuse of patents did not occur, the grip on our economic life which monopoly holds through patents would be a threat to our system of enterprise. The spirit and substance of free enterprise cannot exist in an environment where an independent businessman with an independent idea, or an inventor with a new discovery in a monopoly-ridden field, finds himself compelled either to submit to monopoly control or to be barred from the market. It is ironical but true that while a patent is supposed to give protection and encouragement to the inventor, possession of a patent today is little more than an invitation to predatory litigation. The threat of expensive and protracted patent litigation is perhaps the most effective means by which monopoly enforces its private rule on industry to eliminate competition.

The small businessman facing such obstacles has limited choices of action. He can sue the large group, or risk suit, but in either event will find himself involved in a costly, lengthy process. He generally emerges with a broken spirit and a petition in bankruptcy.

The files of the Department of Justice are crowded with complaints and pleadings of these little men. They have found these handicaps insuperable in their attempts to compete. In giving testimony before the Temporary National Economic Committee, one small manufacturer in the glass container industry recited a tale which is frequently and tragically repeated throughout many branches of production. This particular witness, sued for infringement on nine or ten counts, stated:

"We naturally were finally forced to hire a patent attorney. We had to acquire the services of a Texas attorney, and I think there are some two or three patent attorneys in the State. They brought us into court in April of 1935, as I recall. Well, when I arrived in San Angelo and met them there in the hotel, I can conservatively say there was a half train load of attorneys and equipment. There were motion picture projectors and attorneys all over the place. I don't know anyone of the Hartford legal staff that was not there. They were prepared to give us a nice battle. Well, I had only one attorney and he was considerably lost in that crowd. I wish you might have seen his face that morning. So I promptly asked for a recess until the afternoon in order to see if we couldn't settle the case out of court."

As the witness testified at the time, the "settlement" was "a sort of slow death arrangement."

This situation has become a common condition, but it is not new. Thomas Edison once stated that patent litigation cost him more than he ever made from an invention. Unfortunately, the government has not as yet developed any procedure to protect the legitimate rights which a patent is supposed to confer on the little man. I have hopes that this aspect of the problem will be considered and met in the not too distant future.

Even if every other charge of malpractice or problem of monopolistic abuse of patents were ignored, there would remain a crucial question. Technology is an index of national security, and technological strength depends upon technological freedom. Yet, in two world wars we have learned that the infiltration of American industry by foreign and hostile interests has been conducted through patents and patent agreements.

In 1914, we experienced severe and crippling scarcities of dyestuffs and medicines, because patents held by German interests had prevented the development of American production. In the case of salvarsan, Ehrlich's "magic bullet" for the cure of syphilis, we found that a patent protected the product, but did not reveal the method of its manufacture. The same situation occurred in other drugs, such as veronal and novocaine, and in other fields, such as metal alloys and special electrical equipment.

Since the outbreak of the present war, our vulnerability to this method of attack has been revealed once more. The use of patents as the spearheads of attack in industrial and economic warfare, intended to weaken our war potential, is illustrated in the beryllium industry, in synthetic rubber, in pharmaceuticals, in optical goods, and in other important military and civilian supplies. It is clear that abuses of this nature, having consequences which affect both our national security and our standards of living, cannot be tolerated.

Whether at the hands of domestic or foreign interests, misuse of the patent system and abuses of patent power militate against the best interest of the American people. It is our task and our responsibility to uproot these malpractices. Within the space of four years the Antitrust Division of the Department of Justice has brought more than forty cases involving these typical abuses, and this Division is investigating many more.

I should like it clearly understood that I believe the patent system in many respects has served this country well. As long as it stays within its proper orbit it can continue as a great force in the industrial and scientific development of our country. Indeed, it must be one of our aims to strengthen the patent system to make it more effective for the protection of small business and for the encouragement of new invention. Those who have a deep belief in the patent system should support the government's action in uprooting and eliminating the abuses which have done so much to discredit the patent system generally.

The vigorous enforcement of the antitrust laws is, of course, our greatest guarantee that democratic opportunity will be kept alive in our economic system. Something more is needed, however, to make certain that free enterprise has a fighting chance. In this connection, it is encouraging to note that the Senate has had under consideration legislation intended to provide access to technology to government and public alike. It is, of course, absolutely necessary in the present stage of technological development, where the military security of the nation may well depend upon the quality of its technology, that the government have every facility at its disposal to keep abreast of technological change. From the standpoint of economic health, however, means must be found of granting to the small businessman or the small inventor, who cannot hope to compete on an equal footing with the massive strength and enormous resources of great industrial laboratories, a chance to initiate and develop new ideas, new processes and new products.

In numerous instances patents have been used to discourage research by independent inventors and businessmen. What incentive is there to inventors to develop new products or processes when they may be, in effect, inventing themselves into a patent infringement suit? Very often in such cases the fact of infringement is never determined. We all know that patent litigation is costly and time consuming. In disputes between monopoly groups and smaller opponents the difference in economic strength between the two parties is usually the determining factor. In this situation small competitors often find it less expensive to depend upon the research and the largesse of great corporations, by accepting licenses which are usually restrictive. Under such conditions neither the opportunity nor the fact of free enterprise can flourish.

Conduct of research by government does not mean that it would enter into competition with industry. Rather, research sponsored and carried on with the facilities and support of the government would constitute a strong stimulus to private initiative.

The government would enter no business as a result of carrying on research. It would sell nothing, and it would not prevent others from going into business. The fruits of discoveries produced by government research would be open to all. It is primarily those interests which seek to deny access to technology by independent enterprise that are opposed to the entry of government into this field.

The great need of small business in the post-war world for new opportunities and new directions cannot be fulfilled if the small businessman is denied access to technology. If the government provided the scientific and technical resources which placed small enterprise on an equal footing with great corporations, we should undoubtedly witness a revival of the spirit of industrial adventure.

Ultimately, the entire public as consumers would receive the benefits of a government research program. When competition is absent and research is dominated by monopoly groups, the consumer not only pays higher prices for what he does get, but has no assurance that he is obtaining the best possible products. Monopoly has no incentive to progress, and so long as it is able to control research it need not strive to make better products at lower prices.

In addition to meeting the needs of small business and consumers, the maintenance of scientific research by an over-all public agency is a direct concern of government. The importance of technology to national welfare has been shown strikingly during the present war. There are many areas of scientific research and development which private industry cannot adequately explore and develop. There are many branches of science and technology, as well as of industrial development, where government cannot afford to be dependent upon the efforts of private monopoly groups. The lists of shortages which hampered our war effort in early days of the present struggle resulted in nearly every instance from restrictive effects of monopoly control. Government was forced to turn to monopoly groups which dominated the market. It is essential for the future that the hazard of dependence on monopoly be removed.

Industry itself, large as well as small, would profit tremendously if research conducted by the government supplemented private efforts and increased our stock of scientific knowledge. The creation of new industries would open up new channels for private investment and would help to eliminate the periodic effects of depression. The constant flow of new ideas into industry is essential if we wish to have both full production and full employment. Government research could become one of the principal means of stimulating and encouraging new industry and at the same time overcoming the effects of the business cycle.

The means of correcting patent abuses and of renewing competitive opportunity in industry are available in existing law and with relatively minor modifications in the scope of governmental authority. Unless we are willing to accept private industrial government as a substitute for a free economy, it must be our determination that the spirit and purpose of the patent laws and the conditions necessary to competition shall be securely established. If we would avoid the destruction of the patent system as the consequence of its abuse, it must be made clear to monopoly groups and industry that they cannot base their restrictive practices and policies on patent privileges.

5

Medicines

In a very real sense the producers and distributors of medical products occupy a position of public responsibility. On the whole, those in the drug industry who are charged with this responsibility have carried out their obligations in a highly praiseworthy manner. They are to be commended and congratulated.

In nearly every instance in which the standards of service and of public welfare have not been maintained we find that monopoly groups have been responsible for the abuse of public confidence. When monopoly is able to impose restrictive conditions on the production, the price and the distribution of vital medicines and to determine who may buy and sell products, it is in the interests of the drug industry and the public alike for government to intervene.

Thus when it was found that a small ring of producers had been able to maintain fixed prices on insulin and to pick and choose those who would be allowed to distribute insulin to the public, it was necessary for the government to act.

There are approximately two million persons in the United States suffering from diabetes. Most of these sufferers require one or more daily injections of insulin. They are dependent for their very lives on an adequate supply of the drug at a reasonable price. Yet a monopoly group exploiting its privileged position took advantage of the industry and of the public to impose arbitrary prices and unreasonable conditions of distribution. Wholesalers, distributors, and retailers were compelled to adhere to the edicts of the monopoly group under the threat that if they did not do so, no insulin would be sold to them.

The possible consequences of this exercise of monopoly power on the well-being of victims of diabetes are appalling, yet in the hands of monopoly the needs of the public become subordinated by the edicts which are imposed on the industry and the public alike. It is for this reason that the industry itself, as well as government, must continuously be vigilant to oppose the growth and exercises of monopoly power and to stimulate wholesome competition.

Few effects of monopoly have been more insidious than the consequences of cartel control over many areas in the drug and medical field.

Because of cartel and patent agreements which carve up world markets and divide fields of production, American drug manufacturers have in some cases been denied the right and the chance to develop the American drug industry to its full possibilities. Because international cartels have been able to set up their own trade restrictions, American drug manufacturers have been prevented from competing within the United States. In many cases American manufacturers have been barred from engaging in competition in other countries and from exporting to such countries. In particular, American producers have found themselves shut off from South American markets. Illegal patent abuses and agreements have in other cases prohibited American manufacturers from entering production or carrying on research in many important fields dominated by foreign interests.

The fight against disease is a primary concern of society everywhere. Yet the brilliance and the industry of modern scientists have all too often been perverted by the efforts of selfish groups to fasten the grip of monopoly on products essential to health and welfare. There have been numerous illustrations of the malignant effects of monopoly on national health and on the maintenance of free enterprise in the pharmaceutical industry. It is instructive to recall some of the more flagrant examples of the abuse of monopoly power in the drug and medical field.

The cartel spirit in the pharmaceutical field is exemplified by the following paragraph, written in July 1938 by the German company, I. G. Farbenindustrie:

"There is an agreement between German and Swiss firms of the Chemical Pharmaceutical Industry for the protection of original preparations which are marketed by the individual members of the group. . . . This agreement provides that products which compete with the original products of members of the association and their subsidiaries or affiliated firms shall not be introduced in any country throughout the world."

This agreement may be described as a conspiracy to deprive the world of the benefits of research in new drug products wherever such benefits may conflict with the vested interests of any of the participating drug manufacturers.

The present war is not the first period of crisis in which the United States has found itself dependent for many vitally needed drugs and medicines on cartels dominated by foreign interests.

During the first World War, scarcity of salvarsan, of veronal, of novocaine, and similar synthetic medical products seriously affected the health of our people. It was not until after the war was over that we were able to relieve some of these shortages. In the years between the World War and the present global war cartel interests once more were able to establish their monopolistic control over new pharmaceutical products.

The myth of German superiority in the production of organic medical compounds has been dispelled for many years. It is necessary, however, to recall that this prestige rested not on superior skill but on the abuse of monopoly and patent privileges. A well-known instance of the way in which the German cartel interests sought to exploit their monopoly position is the story of Bayer 205, sometimes called Germanin. Shortly after the end of the World War I. G. Farben announced that it had discovered a cure for sleeping sickness, the disease which is so prevalent in Africa. The Germans refused to reveal the formula for Bayer 205. Instead they sought to use their discovery as the basis of an exchange of the secret process in return for the restoration of Germany's lost colonies. While this bold attempt to balance medical achievement against political advantage is an extreme case, it nevertheless reflects a cartel attitude.

From the standpoint of the progress and growth of the American drug industry it must be realized that the influence of cartels has been the principal factor in keeping American products from world markets. Foreign concerns, by making treaties with monopoly groups in the American drug industry, have been able to monopolize practically the entire continent of South America. One typical agreement between an American corporation and a German concern divided the world market for more than 400 pharmaceutical and chemical products into non-competitive areas. Among the fields included in the agreement were quinine derivatives, sulfa drugs, vitamins and narcotics. The American firm was prohibited from exporting. This same pattern of restriction by which American producers were barred from selling to South America has been found in a whole roster of cartel agreements involving pharmaceutical products. The effects of these agreements have severely handicapped our good neighbor relations with South America and have made more difficult the establishment of healthy trade between the United States and Latin American countries.

If we are to succeed in our efforts to create a better postwar world, it should be evident that we must uproot every vestige of illegal monopoly control over products essential to the health and welfare of our people. Whether the restriction stems from the efforts of a cartel to confine American industry to the domestic market, or to strangle research and production by American concerns, or to use patents to impose unlawful restraints on trade in the drug industry, it must be our determined purpose to restore free enterprise in the pharmaceutical field. Given freedom of opportunity and the incentive to enter branches of the industry heretofore dominated by cartel interests, we may rest assured that American drug manufacturers will demonstrate their outstanding capabilities in research and their ability to compete both at home and abroad. Competition will benefit the American drug industry and permit it to attain its maximum development. What is perhaps even more important, this country will be assured that in the future the health and welfare of its citizens will not be dependent upon the arbitrary exercise of monopoly power.

I am sure that responsible persons in the pharmaceutical industry will not argue that European technology in this field is so superior to ours that competition is futile. If American manufacturers have free access to technology and are not barred by the misuse of patents and the resurrection of cartel arrangements, then the industry will find itself in a healthier financial and technological position as well as in a position more fully to discharge its obligations to the American people. The myth of European superiority in the medical field has been carefully nurtured by foreign interests which have used this propaganda as a commercial device. Only free competition and free enterprise can fully dispel this myth. This cannot be done, however, unless the pharmaceutical industry sees to it that victims of diabetes, malaria, pellagra, rickets and arthritis are not at the mercy of privileged groups who have abused public confidence and exploited human suffering.

The laboratories of our pharmaceutical industry have brought forth wonderful discoveries. Their achievements have been a boon to the human race. But they have a responsibility to erase the blemish caused by those few who have misused their economic power to violate their trust.

The promotion of public welfare as well as the best interests of the pharmaceutical industry are served when research, production and distribution are carried on free from the taint of monopoly. National health, like national economic well-being, demands that freedom of opportunity to conduct research, to engage in business, and to compete in domestic and foreign markets be preserved. No compromise with monopoly control is possible in an industry which is so directly concerned with human welfare.

6

Synthetic Hormones

The use of synthetic hormones in the United States has grown to such an extent that the annual sales amount to many millions of dollars. Something more than half of the entire business in this country has been carried on by four companies. Each of these companies is the subsidiary or affiliate of a corresponding company in Europe. The European companies belong to a hormone cartel which has controlled the hormone business most effectively abroad and in the United States.

After investigating the ramifications of the cartel's activities in this country the Department of Justice prosecuted the four American companies for violations of the antitrust laws. Pleas of nolo contendere were entered by the four corporations and by five of their officials and fines totalling $54,000 were assessed and paid. At the same time, on December 17, 1941, the defendants consented to the entry of a decree in a civil action brought by the government, which enjoined them from further activities in violation of the antitrust laws.

These are the basic aspects of the hormone cartel:

1. Research has been seriously affected by restrictions imposed by foreign cartel members.

2. German interests have entered into patent licensing arrangements with American affiliates under which they—the latter—agreed to withhold their products from Latin American markets.

3. During the war American companies have aided their German affiliates in evading the British blockade.

4. American companies have participated in the use of paper corporations and dummy consignees to avoid the effects of the Black List in Latin America.

5. American concerns have devised deceptive labels to preserve markets for their German affiliates and to aid the spread of German propaganda in Latin America.

6. Members of the cartel have misused patents in schemes to camouflage flagrant violations of the laws of the nation.

7. The recognized benefits which might be obtained by the widespread use of hormones have been to a large extent curtailed by reason of the restrictions and illegal policies of the cartel members.

8. In the case of one of the synthetic hormones, there is evidence indicating that it may have a substantial contribution to make in connection with treatment of wounded soldiers for shock. The cartel restrictions have had their effect upon the production and wide use of this hormone as well as the others.

9. Two of the American companies have been taken over by the Alien Property Custodian and one of these has been sold.

The following explanation of the nature of hormones does not purport to be a scientific discussion. It represents my understanding of the subject based upon what I believe to be reliable authority. I merely give it for what it may be worth as background for the discussion of this cartel.

Hormones are the secretions of certain ductless glands. As they enter the bloodstream they regulate chemically practically every function of the human body. They are really special agents of chemical coordination of the body. They regulate, order and correlate bodily functions with the same precision as that achieved by the nervous system. Since their first definite isolation by the great English physiologists, Bayliss and Starling, in the early years of this century, there has grown up a whole new field of research. Infinitely small amounts of certain hormones have the most profound effects upon the human body and its emotions. As in the case of vitamins, much of our present knowledge is the result of observing the striking pathological defects and abnormalities produced by excess or deficiency of hormones.

Thus deficiency of certain of these drug-like substances from the small thyroid gland causes a marked decrease in metabolism and mental and physical sluggishness. Excess of this same hormone, or complex of substances, has the opposite effect, increasing oxidation and pulse rate, and causing nervousness and emaciation. It also has striking effects upon growth and development. Deficiency in children results in dwarfism and idiocy.

Other hormones such as those from the anterior lobe of the pituitary gland affect the growth of bone. Hormones from the adrenal glands, located near the kidneys, cause constriction of blood vessels, accelerate the heart beat and cause discharge of glucose from the liver. Insulin, one of the most widely known of the hormones, plays an essential role in the metabolism of carbohydrates. Its absence causes diabetes which is characterized by a failure of normal carbohydrate metabolism.

Medical investigators and chemists have been exploring this vast new field of research for many years. They have learned more and more about the actions and composition of these complex substances. For many years they have worked with the extracts from the glands of certain animals to obtain the hormone itself, or as much of it as could be saved in the process of extraction. At the same time they have been analyzing the composition of the hormones, and endeavoring to synthesize the active principles. Among those which have been produced in synthetic form are the male sex hormone, testosterone; the follicular and corpus luteum, both being female sex hormones; and desoxycorticosterone acetate, a synthetic substance which has effects similar to those of cortin.

Cortin is derived from the cortex of the adrenal glands. There is still some question as to the role which this hormone plays, but there is no doubt that it is essential to life. It apparently affects the metabolism of sodium, potassium, and carbohydrates. This hormone plays an important role in the concentration of body fluids and their distribution between the inside and outside of body cells. The hormone is therefore of some use in diseases or conditions where there occur marked changes in the distribution of the body fluids. Specifically, it means the hormones of the adrenal cortex are useful in the treatment of Addison's disease, where it seems to strike a balance in the intake of salt. It has also been suggested that since surgical shock is associated with unbalance of body fluids, this hormone may be of value in counteracting the shock effects. Shock is so complex a condition, however, that there is no general agreement on the effects of the hormone. However, the hormone, or crystalline preparations possessing hormonal activity, are being used by army surgeons both here and abroad for whatever value they possess.

It is with these and certain other pharmaceutical specialties that the hormone cartel has concerned itself. The cartel is composed of five large European companies: Schering A. G. (Berlin); Ciba (Basle); N. J. Organon (Oss, Holland); C. F. Boehringer & Sons (Mannheim); and Chimio (France). Each of the first four has had a subsidiary or affiliate in this country which has been used to carry out the policies of the European company and of the cartel. I shall describe in some detail the practices which were followed in aiding the German companies to avoid the effect of the British blockade and Black List in Latin America.

The Schering A. G. firm is one of the most important pharmaceutical and chemical manufacturers in Germany. It makes photographic supplies, soaps, cosmetics and many other products. However by far the largest part of its production consists of medicinal specialties and fine chemicals, the former being the more important. It is the largest German exporter of pharmaceutical and medical specialties, specializing in sex hormones, vaccines, remedies for venereal and other contagious diseases, rheumatism, tuberculosis, etc., and also laxatives, anti-acids, opiates, etc. It is also one of the larger German exporters of fine chemicals, laboratory chemicals and plant protection chemicals.

At the time of the first World War, Schering A. G. did comparatively little export business. Its export system, established and carefully developed after 1918, is mainly the result of the work of one man, its former president Dr. Julius Weltzien. This export system spreads over the entire world. The procedure in establishing outlets abroad has been as follows: At first sales are made to all who may wish to buy; then, with increasing turnover, a local firm is made sole agent. When the yearly turnover reaches about $25,000, an expert sent from Berlin is coordinated with the sole agency firm. When the yearly turnover exceeds about $50,000, Schering A. G. sets up a firm of its own, directed by managers sent from Berlin. Germans, or men of German descent, are placed in all key positions, and the remainder of the staff is partly German, partly persons of the country in which the agency is located. The final step is to set up factories in the most important markets which are equipped to ampule the finished solutions and to tablet the finished substances which are used in that form. The supervision of all firms abroad is strongly centralized in Berlin.

Until recently, Schering A. G. was one of the largest sellers of pharmaceutical and medicinal specialties in South and Central America. Testimony before the Truman Committee indicated that approximately one-third of all materials shipped into South America by airmail over the German controlled *Lati* airline, during a six months period in 1941, were chemical and pharmaceutical products. Approximately the same amount of books, maps, etc., intended for espionage and propaganda work was also shipped by air since it was the only means of avoiding the British blockade. On the return trips four-fifths of the air cargoes were of mica for the Nazi war machine and most of the remaining fifth was made up of other important war materials. The important role played by the pharmaceutical exports in providing the exchange for purchase of war materials should not be overlooked.

The interruption of exports due to the war caused Schering A. G. to adopt several different methods of continuing its foreign business. Prior to the invasion of Belgium and Holland, firms in those countries and in the Scandinavian countries were used as blinds to avoid the British blockade. Before Italy entered the war, the Milan factory was utilized as a point from which the German goods, labeled in Italy, could be sent out to the rest of the world.

The final step was to transfer to the United States the business of supplying the markets cut off by the blockade. In preparation for this emergency, several measures had been taken long before the actual outbreak of the war.

The center of the new supply system was Schering Corporation (Bloomfield, New Jersey), a firm now held by the U. S. Alien Property Custodian. This firm was established as a Schering A. G. subsidiary in 1929 to manufacture medical specialties for the market in this country. Differing from most other Schering factories outside Germany it developed the finished solutions and substances out of raw or semi-manufactured imported materials, where the others merely finished the process by placing the material in ampule, tablet and package form. Gradually extending its research, laboratory and manufacturing facilities it came to be as fully equipped to manufacture, although on a much smaller scale, all Schering medical specialties as Schering A. G. itself.

All of the common stock of this New Jersey corporation was owned by Chemical and Pharmaceutical Enterprises, Ltd. (Chepha) and held in the name of a nominee of the Swiss Bank. Chepha was owned 51 per cent by the Swiss Bank and 49 per cent by other related interests. However, it has recently come to light that the transaction in 1937 by which Chepha and the Swiss Bank got apparent control of the Schering Corporation, included an option agreement which made it possible for Schering A. G. to regain its interest at any time it so desired. Obviously the transaction was a mere sham to make it appear that the American corporation was controlled from Switzerland rather than from Germany. Actually Schering A. G. had never ceased to exercise its domination over Schering Corporation up to the very outbreak of war between Germany and the United States.

As of January 1, 1938 the two corporations entered into an extensive and detailed agreement. Two paragraphs of the preamble of this agreement are as follows:

"Schering A. G. is engaged in the development, manufacture and/or sale of medicinal, pharmaceutical, biological, and bacteriological preparations. It is the owner of processes and formulae used in the production of such preparations and is also the owner of U. S. A. patents and patent applications pertaining to such preparations. For many years it has maintained and operated and still does maintain and operate laboratories to carry on research and development work in connection with such preparations, and has thereby acquired valuable scientific knowledge, data and material concerning the aforesaid sphere of activities.

"Schering Corp. has an organization suited for national distribution and promotion of such preparations in the United States of America, and is equipped to manufacture such preparations. It also maintains and operates laboratories to carry on research and development work in connection with such preparations, but has not acquired the extensive scientific knowledge and practical experience in this field that Schering A. G. commands by reason of its longer and more extensive research work and experience."

This language portrays the true relationship of the parent and subsidiary companies.

The parties agreed to exchange patents and information and to deal in each other's products in their respective territories. The division of territory, as in so many of these German-American agreements, gave the United States to the American corporation as its territory and the remainder of the world to the German firm.

Article V, Paragraph 5 is as follows:

"Schering A. G. agrees not to deal in selected preparations nor to sell selected preparations to any corporation or person in the U. S. A. except to Schering Corp., nor knowingly to sell them to any corporation or person for purposes of exportation to or resale in the U. S. A. unless Schering Corp. shall first have given its written consent."

Article V, Paragraph 7 is as follows:

"Schering Corp. undertakes not to export, either directly or indirectly, from the U. S. A., or knowingly to sell for purposes of export to any third party any such preparations unless Schering A. G. shall have previously given its written consent."

A letter from Schering Corporation to Schering A. G. dated June 2, 1939 contained the following:

"In view of your assignment to us of certain patents in the female-sex-hormone field and your assistance in connection with the acquisition by us of licenses under patents in the male-sex-hormone and cortin fields, we agree not to sell or offer for sale any product made pursuant to the said assigned and/or licensed patents or any of them in any country outside of the U. S."

All Schering A. G. patents and trademarks in the United States are owned by Schering Corporation or its affiliates. However, the agreement is not limited in its terms to the mere fixing of compensation for the use of patents and trademarks. The American corporation agreed to pay Schering A. G. a royalty on all its sales of pharmaceutical products which had nothing to do with Schering A. G. patents and trademarks. It even went so far as to agree to pay the German firm a royalty of not to exceed 12½ per cent on sales of new preparations developed by itself in this country. The following provisions of Article X of the agreement make clear this unusual relationship:

"In either of such cases [if net sales of Saraka, a proprietary laxative, are more or less than $1,200,000] the royalty shall be as follows:

"(b) On that portion of such amount derived from sales of preparations commonly available in the open market and not sold under a trademark, such as insulin, milk of magnesia, thyroid, or codliver oil, and in the manufacture of which no special Schering A. G. process is utilized, 6¼%;

(c) On that portion of such amount derived from sales of new preparations developed by Schering Corp. wholly independent of Schering A. G. and which do not fall within a field of preparations already developed or in process of development by Schering A. G., a percentage, less than 12½%, to be determined and agreed upon by the parties from time to time."

Up to the outbreak of the war there was a constant exchange of experience and knowledge by frequent mutual visits. This differs radically from the conditions which prevailed in many other fields. In the case of synthetic rubber for instance, the Hitler government flatly prohibited the giving out of technical information while using every means of securing the information of developments in this country. It seems obvious that in the case of Schering A. G., the plan, as subsequently carried out, was to place Schering Corporation in a position of being able to carry on Schering A. G.'s overseas business. In this rapidly changing field of hormones, this meant keeping the American corporation completely informed as well as getting from it all available information.

Schering Corporation, before the outbreak of war, was provided with complete instructions about the technicalities of exporting Schering products, with a complete set of Schering export packages, labels, prescriptions, etc., indicating all details of the complicated system of packages which differ from country to country and from product to product. This was done to enable Schering Corporation to start exporting without delay in case of emergency. For these products, which before the war had not been made by Schering Corporation, the necessary manufacturing directions were sent from Berlin. About these products until as recently as 1941 there was a constant exchange between Bloomfield and Berlin.

In addition to establishing a "neutral" manufacturer and supplier in the United States which in case of emergency could be resorted to as a new center of the overseas business, Schering A. G. took other measures as well. The Schering subsidiary in London, Schering, Ltd., was also sold to Chepha. It is understood that it has since been or is being wound up by the British government. Shortly before the outbreak of the war in 1939, all Schering A. G. firms in the British Empire, except London, and those in Latin America, were transferred to Foreign Investments and Invention Company, Ltd. Basle (Forinvent.) This was done to "neutralize" these Schering firms and thus to protect them from seizure in the British Empire or blacklisting in Latin America. Forinvent is wholly owned by Palladium A. G., also a Swiss holding company, which in turn is wholly owned by the Swiss Bank Corporation, Basle. Forinvent, like Chepha, is within the premises and organization of the Swiss Bank. The president is the same Dr. Samuel Schweitzer of the Swiss Bank, who is in charge of Chepha, and the connections of Forinvent and Chepha with the Swiss Bank are practically identical. Due to the fact that the selling transaction in the case of Forinvent took place immediately before the outbreak of war, Forinvent could not escape being placed on the blacklist. The same holds true for the Forinvent (Schering A. G.) subsidiaries in Latin America, while the Forinvent (Schering A. G.) subsidiaries in the British countries were placed under enemy alien control.

The carefully laid plans were put into effect upon the outbreak of war. Forinvent advised the British Empire companies to get their further supplies from Schering Corporation and at the same time advised the latter to supply them, which it did.

The fact that the British government acted quickly and placed Forinvent and its subsidiaries in Latin America on the blacklist partially upset the plans which had been made. In view of the increasing anti-German attitude in the United States and the possibility of this country entering the war sooner or later, Schering Corporation had to be very careful of its outward connections with the Schering A. G. set-up. Therefore when Schering Corporation was finally advised to supply Latin America, steps were taken to conceal any connections with the blacklisted Forinvent firms. On January 2, 1940 Schering A. G. gave a release to Schering Corporation as to all products excepting hormones, and on March 1, 1940, cabled a blanket release in the following terms: "We authorize you until further notice to deliver pharmaceutical and technical chemicals to our South and Central American representatives or through their mediation to their customers." These releases, of course, did not apply to foreign firms not associated with Schering A. G., and evidence shows that the restrictions as to these other companies were still continued, and Schering Corporation refused to sell to them.

Two paper corporations were created to avoid use of the name Schering although both corporations are in the same building with Schering Corporation and are completely identified with it except as to name. Pharmex, Inc., owned by Gregory Stragnell, vice president of Schering Corporation, dealt directly with the ex-Schering A. G. subsidiaries in the British Empire, except Schering Corporation, Limited, of Canada. The latter deals directly with Schering Corporation of Bloomfield.

Delta Pharmaceutical Corporation, owned by Sherka Chemical Company (which was in turn owned by Chepha), purchased raw materials from Sherka and hormone products from Schering Corporation and sold them to Atlantis, a corporation organized in Panama. These two companies, Pharmex and Delta, were really the export department of Schering Corporation. Part of their employees were on the pay roll of Schering and part on the pay rolls of Pharmex, Delta and Sherka. Both companies were under the direction of Dr. Weltzien and Dr. Stragnell, then president and vice president, respectively, of Schering Corp.

Atlantis S. A., Panama, is a wholly owned subsidiary of Forinvent organized in 1940. Its president is Dr. Samuel Schweitzer, who is likewise in charge of Chepha and Forinvent. At first it was considered advisable to set up an actual office in Panama. However since so many technical questions, passport difficulties and tax questions were involved, the whole Atlantis business was centralized in Basle, Switzerland, under the direct supervision of the Swiss Bank Corporation, in closest cooperation with Schering A. G. of Berlin.

One of the problems faced by Schering Corporation in its new foreign trade was that of packaging and labeling the products so that they would seem to be identical with those formerly supplied by Schering A. G. Since one of the chief considerations prompting this whole scheme was preservation of good will, in order that the business could be turned back to Schering A. G. after the war, this factor was most important. On February 10, 1940 Forinvent cabled Pharmex as follows: "fundamental changes of packing latinamerica may jeopardize turnover on account customers mentality and will probably cause difficulties with registration authorities therefore please adopt present style of packing and labeling . . . suggest airmailing you immediately films for making plates [for printing Schering A. G. type of labels]." It was not necessary to use the films in question inasmuch as Delta had samples of all the Latin America packages it had used as a standard pattern. Delta on January 28, 1941, sent to Swiss Bank samples of all packages used for export, pointing out that the differences between the new and old packages were very slight.

From early in 1940 until Pearl Harbor the supplying of Schering A. G. firms in Latin America was accomplished in a circuitous manner. Each of the firms kept in close touch with Basle and so with Berlin. They advised Atlantis of their requirements. Atlantis, in Basle, cabled the orders to Delta at Bloomfield and instructed Swiss Bank in New York to honor Delta's drafts. Delta delivered the goods to a forwarding agent of Atlantis in New York, which shipped them to a dummy consignee in Latin America and they were there received by the particular Schering firm which had placed the order.

About 40 or 45 cents of each dollar paid by the Latin American firm went to Atlantis and thus to Schering A. G. Out of its share, 55 or 60 cents, Delta (actually Schering Corporation) made its manufacturing costs and whatever profit there might be for it. The advertising expense was borne by Atlantis or Schering A. G. The advertising and continuance of the familiar German packages, labels and Schering trade-mark constituted an important form of German propaganda. It was possible for the German agents in Latin America to point to the continuance of German pharmaceutical supplies as indicative of their ability to overcome the British blockade and to carry on their commerce with this hemisphere.

It has been mentioned that the Germans used pharmaceuticals which have a high value in proportion to bulk and weight to make up one third of the air cargoes which were flown into South America along with propaganda and other materials. Pharmaceuticals also constituted an important part of the air cargo which was carried eastward, ranking third among the materials which were flown over the blockade. One order of 10 kilos (22 pounds) of testosterone propionate, the semi-manufactured male hormone, valued at $50,000 was shipped one kilo a week by air mail from Argentina to Spain and from there to the Schering factory at either Milan or Berlin. This and other similar orders, were placed by a dummy of Schering

A. G. in Portugal.

Thus far I have been discussing the relations of two firms, one, the largest of the European manufacturers of synthetic hormones, and the other its affiliate or subsidiary, the largest American producer. There are other large European members of the cartel and each has its subsidiary in this country.

Ciba (Society of Chemical Industry in Basle, Switzerland) is another important cartel member. It has been in existence for some sixty years, engaged in the manufacture and sale of dyestuffs and pharmaceutical products throughout the world. In July 1936 it organized a subsidiary, Ciba Pharmaceutical Products, Inc., of Summit, New Jersey. Ciba Basle also came to own several other corporations in fields other than pharmaceuticals and hormones in this country, and companies in Canada, Brazil and Argentina which sell dyestuffs and pharmaceuticals. Ciba's close relation to Schering A. G. is indicated by its joint ownership with the Swiss Bank of the common stock of Chepha, which in turn owns all the common stock of Schering Corporation.

Until just before the war Ciba Pharmaceutical of Summit, New Jersey, produced no hormone products. These were all purchased by it from Ciba Basle. However, since its organization it has been distributing hormones under its own label.

The subservient attitude of Ciba Summit to the Society (Ciba, Basle) is clearly shown in the following paragraph from a letter of October 17, 1939, from H. Kamp, vice president of the New Jersey corporation, to James Brodbeck, Secretary of Ciba Basle:

"As I have repeatedly said, I am not interested in making profits for Summit out of sales of raw materials or even finished packages sent to foreign countries. *All I am interested in is to help Society in getting the business*, but we must have a certain rule as regards profits for Summit. The simplest way would be if Basle fixed a percentage profit over our price II on all products shipped in bulk to any foreign country. The same, of course, could apply to finished packages if we were to supply finished packages to foreign countries later on. *We want to help Society as I fully realize that we are working for the interest of Society and not for the interest of Ciba Summit alone. Whatever seems most advantageous from your point of view will meet with my approval."*

The same attitude is also reflected in a letter of September 22, 1939 from H. Kamp of Ciba Summit to Dr. J. Weltzien, president of Schering Corporation:

"At the meeting which took place on May 10, 1939 in your offices, among other points, the introduction of desoxycorticosterone acetate was discussed. It was finally agreed that Ciba would introduce the product, but would abide by your suggestion that no other indications be mentioned in the literature than Addison's Disease. We were, therefore, more than surprised to read your advertisement in the 'Druggists Circular' announcing 'CORTATE,' where it is suggested that the drug may be of use in the more chronic constitutional types of cortical deficiency, in asthenias, and that certain allergies should be benefited by the administration of Cortate. . . .

"It is again one of your usual methods by putting the other parties before accomplished facts. I have discussed your tactics very thoroughly while in Basle, and I can assure you that our friends in Basle are more than fed up with your *methods. In fact, I have the full authority to give you a dose of your own medicine at the next opportunity, and this I am going to do without any hesitation whatsoever!"*

N. V. Organon of Oss, Holland, is a large manufacturer of hormone products and so is F. Hoffman-LaRoche of Basle, Switzerland. The latter company has had a subsidiary in Nutley, New Jersey called Hoffman-LaRoche, Inc. N. V. Organon of Oss and Hoffman-LaRoche, Inc., of Nutley, have jointly owned a corporation called Roche-Organon, Inc., organized in 1937 and engaged in the sale of hormones. In 1940 Ciba licensed Roche-Organon to manufacture products in the cortin field under a patent for which it had made application in 1938. Ciba agreed to pay Roche-Organon 20 per cent of all royalties collected from other licensees except Schering. Roche-Organon agreed to pay Ciba 6 per cent on its entire turnover in the United States in the Cortin field from January 1, 1940 to June 17, 1955 regardless of whether the turnover involved products made under Ciba's patent.

The German firm of C. F. Boehringer and Sons of Mannheim-Waldhof, Germany formerly owned 50 per cent of the stock of Rare Chemicals, Inc., Nepera Park, New York. The president of the German firm was the father of E. T. Fritzsching, formerly secretary and more recently president of Rare Chemicals. A memorandum of the younger Fritzsching of Rare, dated March 29, 1939, contains the following opening paragraph:

"In view of the boycott situation and in view of a number of other reasons I have come to the conclusion that the best way to avoid any further trouble for Rare Chemicals is to arrange for a definite purchase of the Boehringer shares by an American citizen. It is my intention to make an offer to Boehringer, by which I shall take over their assets in this country and pay for them at whatever price I could possibly obtain them. I am assuming this obligation personally for the reason that it really makes very little difference whether the shares are owned by Boehringer or by me, since through this transaction the assets would morally still remain within the same family interests. It would also work along the lines of my personal interest and that of my family in the event of war."

The remaining 50 per cent of Rare's stock was owned by Pyridium Corporation also of Nepera Park, New York. A letter to Erwin Fritzsching c/o C. F. Boehringer & Soehne, G.m.b.H., Mannheim-Waldhof from W. S. Lasdon of Pyridium and president of Rare dated August 18, 1939 contained the following statement: "I agree with your suggestion to the transfer of the B.&S. stock to a Swiss Company, instead of to you, and of course, your participation in the profits of Rare is to be cancelled upon the signing of this agreement, the understanding being that you and W. S. Lasdon will represent the stockholding interests." The products of the two companies were exchanged with definite restrictions upon their distribution. The following excerpt indicates that the German firm kept a tight rein on the use by the American firm of the former's products. It is taken from a letter from Fritzsching of C. F. Boehringer & Soehne, G.m.b.H. to Rare Chemicals, Inc., dated October 31, 1936. It concerns a request of Rare to be allowed to manufacture a product called Eucupin.

"We are acknowledging the receipt of your letter of October 19th and regret to say that we cannot comply with your wishes.

"We must take into consideration also the German interest when weighing the question whether it is right to send manufacturing processes to foreign countries, even though they may go to our friends in these countries. We cannot be responsible for it to give you manufacturing processes, the use of which is not to be expected within a reasonable time. In such a case we cannot truthfully answer any possible questions from authorities to the effect that we can say that when giving away a manufacturing process it will make it possible to manufacture and sell in a foreign country a German preparation, the sale of which from Germany due to duty difficulties and other restrictions cannot be considered. In this fact lies the German interest, and this we have to consider in first line."

In the summer of 1942 Rare was taken over by the Alien Property Custodian and subsequently sold at public auction to a wholly American independent organization.

After certain separate agreements and considerable negotiation a five party agreement was entered into on May 26, 1937 to which the European firms Schering A. G.; Ciba, Basle; N. V. Organon, Oss, Holland; C. F. Boehringer & Sons, and Les Laboratoires Francais de Chimiotherapie of France (Chimio) were the parties. The male hormone, female sex hormones, and cortin, the cortico adrenal hormone, are covered by the agreement. It involved a division of territories with certain parties being definitely excluded from certain territories. Competing producers of pharmaceutical products were expressly named as firms with which any kind of cooperation is prohibited. Among these were E. Merck, Darmstadt, Germany, and Merck & Co., Inc., of Rahway, New Jersey. Subsequent agreements removed the prohibition as to these firms.

Of course, one of the chief purposes of the cartel agreement was to fix prices. The European parties agreed upon prices and their American affiliates did likewise. A memorandum of a meeting held at Summit on October 6, 1938 between representatives of Ciba and of Schering discusses the fixing of prices on various hormones. The artificial and arbitrary character of the pricing policies is indicated by quotations from some of the documents which were written following this meeting. One of them indicates an agreed price of $3 for a certain hormone product. It then states: "This price was later refused by Mr. Kamp [Ciba's general manager] who then advocated $4.00. This was submitted to the other with our O.K."

A memorandum of a discussion held at Bloomfield, New

Jersey on October 7, 1938 between representatives of Rare and of Schering, recites a detailed list of prices agreed upon between Schering and Ciba the preceding day) as having been submitted to Rare.

As to the item on which the price had been changed as just indicated an endorsement on this memorandum states: "Informed Mr. Landon [Rare official] by phone of Summit's desire to change this price to $4. He agreed to this."

The entire world cartel system has been bound together with patents. The contracts among the American companies have been carefully planned and drafted abroad to avoid any appearance of violating the antitrust laws. They were couched in terms of licensing patents to give the impression that the parties were merely procuring rights under patents and not engaging in restraints of competition. The evidence indicates that the cartel participants in Europe had attempted to allocate the issue of patents in the United States to the associated firms in such a manner as to strengthen the defense of the American firms against charges of antitrust law violations. At a discussion in Berlin on March 18, 1939 among representatives of Ciba, Organon, and Schering, A. G. there was set in motion reciprocal concessions of priority in interferences between Organon and Ciba in the U. S. Patent Office relating to the male hormone, and to cortin. It was arranged for Schering to drop out of the interference proceedings. It appears from a circular letter from Organon to Ciba and Schering that the plan was for Organon to concede priority to Ciba in the male hormone interference and for Ciba to concede priority in the interference regarding cortin. The intent of the parties, as to the male hormone interference, was to transfer the application of Organon to the United States Ciba firm. This circular letter of April 4, 1939, from Ciba to Organon and Schering, A. G. reads in part:

"It is up to Ciba to take care in accordance with the several single agreements in the United States for a correct and clear basis of the agreements relating to the male hormone field because corresponding proceedings are intended in the paranephros [cortin] hormone field in which Roche-Organon shall obtain the basic patent claims. In accordance with the opinion expressed here since Ciba gives its consent already in the letter of March 9, 1939 to transfer the basic application in which the patent claims for paranephros are established (Case 1577/1-4) to Roche-Organon, that however, is dependent upon corresponding proceedings of the Organon in the male hormone field."

The reasons for this "swapping" were very clearly indicated in the last mentioned document:

"As it is known in the United States the antitrust legislation is of extremely great significance. The different agreements which are in the state of preparation in the United States are intended to put all contractors into position to sell hormone compounds in the United States without any violation of those statutes. . . . So far as . . . cross promises to maintain prices exist, this promise is only lawful if the licensee, in this case Ciba, possesses the protection of a patent claim . . .

. . . .

"According to the information of Dr. Joseph Engi almost daily new indictments based on the antitrust legislation are made. Under such circumstances it is extremely important to obtain as fast as possible the protection of the most important patent claims."

However, Roche-Organon resisted the transfer of the application, writing in its circular letter to Ciba and Schering, A. G., dated April 15, 1939: "An expert would understand immediately that the transfer of this application served only aims which have to be considered as lawful according to the antitrust legislation. We couldn't even mention any consideration given the Ciba."

Although Organon's male hormone application was in fact not transferred to Ciba, the result which the parties contemplated appears to have been effected. Ciba, apparently relying upon its own male hormone patents in the United States, became the licensor of Roche, Schering, and Rare, while Roche-Organon participated in the licensing arrangements only under its cortin patents.

There are numerous indications in the Schering correspondence that the American license agreements are so bound up with the basic cartel agreements that the sums of money paid by the American firms to each other are regarded as parts of the total considerations which the European firms are bound to pay each other.

As in the case of Schering A. G. and Schering Corporation the other cartel members bound their United States affiliates to agreements which precluded exports in any manner which would interfere with the division of territory among members of the cartel. The agreement of April 1, 1938 between N. V. Organon and Roche-Organon contains the following provisions: "Roche-Organon agrees not to deal in or manufacture glandular and hormone preparations other than those originated by Oss [N. V. Organon], nor to export or sell for export from the territory any glandular and hormone preparations." (The territory is defined as the United States, its territories and possessions, Canada and the Philippine Islands, and Cuba.) The other agreements contain similar restrictions with some variations as to the exact territory.

The principles of competition, price, and research heretofore discussed are well exemplified by the case of Stilbestrol (diethylstilbestrol), a recently discovered pharmaceutical which has effects similar to those of the female sex hormones. It is the product of research supported by Government grant in England, several scientists of the University of London and of Oxford University, headed by E. C. Dodds, being responsible for the development. Throughout all of the work of Dodds and his colleagues the Medical Research Council, a British government organization, undertook the necessary financial support. (While Stilbestrol is not a synthetic hormone, it has most of the valuable therapeutic effects of these substances although it may not be entirely free from side reactions. Its cost of manufacture—and the price to the consumer—are much lower than those of the equivalent hormones).

The American hormone cartel members were aware of Stilbestrol and its possibilities as early as 1939. In a conference of Roche-Organon, Ciba and Schering officials, held on August 1, 1939 the following discussion took place, according to minutes found in Ciba's files:

"Mr. Kamp [Ciba] brought up the subject stilbestrol.

"Mr. Hammer [Schering] said he thought that any concern would have a hard time getting stilbestrol accepted in this country.

"Dr. Oppenheimer [Ciba] pointed out that in this country estradiol prices may not be too much out of line with those of stilbestrol compared with Great Britain.

"The question of side effects from stilbestrol was then discussed.

"Dr. Josephy [Roche-Organon] told of reports from Amsterdam on the use of stilbestrol in animal experimentation. He said that he thought the government would look not only at the favorable reports on a preparation which was submitted but also the unfavorable ones.

"Mr. Kamp said he thought some concern had already filed with the government a request to market stilbestrol."

A memorandum in Schering's file concerning this same conference of August 1, 1939 is somewhat more revealing:

"XVIII *Stilbestrol.* Ciba and Roche-Organon want to have it just to be able to knock it with physicians. They say the hormone business in England has been destroyed just by this new product. On the other hand, it is said to injure the liver and there is doubt that the U. S. Government will allow it to be used."

In the minutes (from Ciba's files) of a conference of representatives of the three companies on Friday, October 27, 1939, there is this statement: "During the discussion Stilbestrol was mentioned and Dr. Weltzien [President of Schering] remarked he hoped 'none of us will introduce Stilbestrol'." These quotations indicate the hostility of cartel members towards a new product which endangers their control of the market. Stilbestrol was put on the market in this country late in 1941 and had an immediate effect upon the sales of the higher priced hormone products.

From what has been said it seems clear that in the field of synthetic hormones the cartel control has been such as to be detrimental to our national interest. When such control can be used to make American corporations the tools of those of other countries it is exceedingly unfortunate. When carried to the point of causing corporations in this country to aid the Axis it could not be and was not tolerated. The seizure of two of these companies by the Alien Property Custodian has put an end to the German control. From the point of view of encouragement of research those two companies are much better off than they were when tied to the apron strings of their parent companies in Germany. Complete removal of cartel restrictions from the entire industry would be definitely in the interest of the general public in this country and throughout the world.

7

Vitamins

The monopolistic control of one of the most essential products of our modern era—the sunshine vitamin, also known as Vitamin D—has been magnified by the fact that it is the poorer elements of our country which have the greatest need for this product, since it is a preventative and a cure for certain diseases most commonly found among the lower economic strata of our population. Vitamin D is essential for proper bone growth and development, the prevention and cure of rickets, and the prevention or reduction of tooth decay.

The Wisconsin Alumni Research Foundation acts as a screen behind which a group of monopolistic chemical, pharmaceutical and food companies control Vitamin D. The story of the Wisconsin Alumni Research Foundation is of extreme importance because it indicates how a quasi-public research organization can be flagrantly misused.

At the outset I should like to state that the Wisconsin Alumni Research Foundation has no formal connection with the University of Wisconsin, and that the University of Wisconsin has absolutely no control over the policies and practices of the Alumni Foundation. It should be clearly understood, therefore, that what I say here does not reflect in any manner upon the University of Wisconsin.

A report of the Trustees of the Foundation dated June 22, 1931, defines the objectives and purposes of the Foundation as follows:

"Indeed one of the soundest reasons for the development of the Foundation as a suitable means of handling the Steenbock process lies in the rigid control through which it is possible to protect the public and prevent unscrupulous commercialism from capitalizing the Steenbock discovery."

The investigation by the Antitrust Division of the Department of Justice indicates, however, that somewhere along the line these laudable objectives were lost. Instead, a summary of our investigation discloses the following facts about the Wisconsin Alumni Research Foundation:

(1) It has been the vehicle for creating a domestic monopoly resulting in division of fields, price fixing, control of container size, and limitation of potency of vitamin products—as a result of which the public has been charged excessive and arbitrarily high prices. (The Foundation has been described by a licensee as being "merciless in beating out competition" in the field of vitamins.)

(2) It has considered plans to denature and adulterate Vitamin D preparations in order to maintain high prices.

(3) It has exhibited a lack of interest in research unless a commercial advantage could be obtained.

(4) It has used threats of patent litigations under patents which it knew were very weak to eliminate competition. (Some of these patents upon which the monopolistic scheme rested were, in fact, declared invalid in 1943 by the Circuit Court of Appeals for the Ninth Circuit.)

(5) It has suppressed the use of competing processes.

(6) It has organized international cartels with I. G. Farben of Germany and Joseph Nathan & Co., of Great Britain, in order to eliminate world competition by dividing world territory into noncompetitive areas.

(7) It has attempted to suppress the publication of scientific research data which were at variance with its monopoly interests.

(8) It has acted as a police organization for its licensees—in order to maintain its price fixing arrangements—by setting up a black list of price-cutting distributors.

(9) It has used its licensing scheme to discourage research by its licensees.

(10) It has endeavored to suppress or prevent truthful advertising in order to eliminate competition.

(11) It has required its licensees to charge unreasonable prices to the government.

(12) It has forced farmers to buy vitamin-enriched animal feeds in a monopoly market.

Since 1925 the production and use of Vitamin D has been under the control of the Wisconsin Alumni Research Foundation. The control has been based upon the so-called Steenbock patents, especially upon patent No. 1680818, which the Foundation regards as the basic patent on Vitamin D.

About 1925 Dr. Steenbock, then a professor at the University of Wisconsin, conducted experiments which eventually resulted in the Steenbock patents. Recognizing the commercial possibilities of his developments, Steenbock offered his patents to the University, but the Regents of the institution did not feel they were in a position to commercialize them. The President of the Wisconsin Alumni Association at that time was George I. Haight, a very able patent lawyer of Chicago, who immediately recognized the commercial possibilities of the Steenbock development. Together with some of the other leading alumni of the University, Haight founded the Wisconsin Alumni Research Foundation to undertake the exploitation of the Steenbock patents and such other patents as the Foundation might from time to time acquire.

The Foundation was chartered on November 14, 1925 as a non-profit corporation. Its purposes, as stated in its charter were "to promote, encourage and aid scientific investigation and research at the University of Wisconsin by the faculty, staff, alumni and students thereof, and those associated therewith, and to provide or assist in providing the means and machinery by which their scientific discoveries, inventions and processes may be developed, applied and patented, and the public and commercial uses thereof determined, and by which such utilization or disposition may be made of such discoveries, inventions and processes, and patent rights or interests therein, as may tend to stimulate and promote and provide funds for further scientific investigation and research within said University or colleges or departments thereof."

The Foundation is managed by a Board of Trustees. Originally these trustees personally handled the work of the Foundation but, in 1931, they secured the services of Henry L. Russell, former dean of the University of Wisconsin College of Agriculture. Russell was made Director and executive head of the Foundation. Later, as business increased, L. D. Barney was employed as business manager, and Ward Ross, an associate of Haight, was retained as General Counsel. Steenbock himself appears to have handled most of the technical matters of the Foundation insofar as they relate to Vitamin D. The royalties received by the Foundation are invested and the resulting income is utilized for research.

The Foundation has controlled Vitamin D by reason of its ownership of the Steenbock patents Nos. 1680818, 1871135,

1871136, and 2057399. The underlying concept of all of these patents is that certain substances called pro-vitamins may be "activated" so as to result in a product having a high Vitamin D potency. This "activation" is accomplished by exposing the pro-vitamin to ultra-violet light, and the basic patent is limited to activation by ultra-violet light produced by an artificial source such as a quartz mercury vapor lamp.

The commercialization of the Steenbock patents was phenomenally successful almost from the very outset. The report of the Trustees of the Foundation dated June 22, 1931, states: "The accumulation from royalties so far has been almost wholly from the ultra-violet patents. During the calendar year 1930, the gross income was $354,590, or very nearly $1,000 a day throughout the year. This income has been developed within less than three years."

The Foundation's annual royalties showed a steady increase until 1936, when they amounted to nearly $1,100,000. After 1936, the annual royalties decreased slightly, and in 1939 they amounted to $936,610.70 or over $2,500 per day. Up to 1940, the Foundation had received more than $8,500,000 in royalties.

The royalty rates charged by the Foundation vary from 10% to 3% and less, with higher royalties applying to only a few products. The enormous size of the market is indicated by the munificent revenues yielded by royalties at these rates.

The first requirement for the success of the Foundation's licensing program was the elimination of competition from non-licensees. The Foundation's practices in this respect are aptly described in a memorandum dated February 20, 1935, from Connolly, a du Pont patent attorney, to Kupperian, of du Pont: "The Foundation has been merciless in beating out competition throughout the United States whenever such competition threatened to encroach upon the synthetic vitamin D field."

Some of the leading manufacturers in the country are licensees of the Foundation. Many of these manufacturers have been licensees for years, while in some cases licenses were obtained by the acquisition of companies holding licenses. Both du Pont and Standard Brands obtained their licenses by the latter method.

Acetol Products, Inc., had a license from the Foundation dated November 15, 1929. Du Pont acquired the assets of Acetol and on April 30, 1935, Acetol assigned its license to du Pont. On November 15, 1935, a new agreement was executed between the Foundation and du Pont which superseded the Acetol agreement of November 15, 1929.

Standard Brands succeeded to the rights of the Fleischmann Company under an agreement dated August 8, 1928.

The question naturally arises why these powerful manufacturers paid the Foundation such large royalties on the basis of the weak and limited Steenbock patents. The correspondence indicates that the licensees were not only willing but anxious to pay the royalties in return for the profit opportunities offered under the Foundation's schemes.

The desire of the licensees to cooperate in the Foundation's promotional schemes is well expressed in a letter dated July 8, 1935, from Atkins of du Pont to Barney, the Foundation's business manager:

"The writer feels certain that you understand our desire and willingness to be considered as a part of the Foundation. You know our desire to prevent the Vitamin D field from falling into disrepute because of too many producers of various types of so-called Vitamin D. We would much prefer centralized control in the hands of the Foundation and you may count on us to support you even though, at times, we may have differences of opinion."

A memorandum dated January 25, 1937, from H. W. Elley, associate chemical director of du Pont, to a number of the executives of du Pont, explains the reason for centralizing "control in the hands of the Foundation":

"He [Mr. Protto, assistant general manager of du Pont] felt that it would be preferable to deal with the Wisconsin Alumni Foundation since they could be of considerable value to the industry in policing and regulating matters. If, for any reason such arrangements become unnecessary, it would then be possible to consider alternative procedures not involving the use of the Foundation patents, that is, we might commercialize the Milas process."

The Foundation is organized along the lines of an international cartel insofar as its licensing program is concerned. It is party to agreements with the omnipresent I. G. Farbenindustrie of Germany and Joseph Nathan & Co., of Britain. The agreements, following the standard cartel pattern, create exclusive noncompetitive territories. Nathan and I. G. are prohibited from exporting to the United States and the domestic licensees of the Foundation are prohibited from exporting to Germany or Great Britain.

The domestic licensing policy of the Foundation is characterized by a most complex and minute division of fields into noncompetitive areas. Generally speaking, these fields of activity are made exclusive so that all competition between the different licensees or groups of licensees is eliminated. Provisions of the various agreements, which will be later described, prevent any substantial overlapping of these fields. Often the provisions merely prohibit the licensee from accurately describing his product but the essential object, elimination of competition, is attained.

Fields are divided along three distinct lines: (a) the product to be activated, (b) the method of activation, and (c) the use of the activated product. In the first category there are 13 principal divisions: (1) the pharmaceutical licensees are permitted to activate ergosterol, (2) Standard Brands is licensed to activate yeast and yeast products, (3) du Pont is allowed to activate ergosterol cholesterol and other sterols except yeast and yeast products, (4) S. S. Kovaks is allowed to activate sterols derived from yeasts but not yeast, (5) a group of licensees are permitted to activate evaporated milk, (6) a number of licensees are permitted to activate fluid milk, (7) Quaker Oats is allowed to activate cereals, (8) Borden is allowed to activate a milk product known as Dryco, (9) The Wanter Company is allowed to activate Ovaltine, (10) the Commander Larrabee Company is allowed to activate flour, (11) R. B. Davis and Company is allowed to activate Cocomalt, (12) Loose-Wiles Biscuit Company is allowed to activate crackers, and (13) Ayerst, McKenna and Harrison are allowed to activate a food product known as Glucose-D.

The extent to which the division of fields is carried is exemplified in an agreement dated June 27, 1938, between the Foundation and the Loose-Wiles Biscuit Company. This agreement authorizes Loose-Wiles to activate "Graham Crackers" and "Wafers slightly sweetened to such as English Style Arrowroot Wafers," but does not permit the activation of "cakes" and "cookies."

According to the method of activation, fields are divided into direct irradiation and activation by the introduction of an irradiated substance. Some few licensees are permitted to use either method of activation, but most are restricted to a single method. One of the most curious licenses issued by the Foundation permits the activation of milk by feeding cows irradiated material.

The division of fields according to use is most detailed, but can be broken into several general classes. Licenses are issued for the human medicine field, for the human food field, for the fluid milk field, for the evaporated milk field, for the animal feed field, and for a field in which the product is not intended for internal use.

At the outset, it was pointed out that the stated objectives of the Foundation are "to protect the public" and "to prevent unscrupulous commercialization." Over the years the Foundation's devotion to these objectives appears to have wavered, The Foundation appears to be primarily interested in royalties, with little or no regard for the public interest. Article VII of the agreement of November 1, 1938, with the milk companies states that if "it should be found that the activation of unsweetened evaporated milk by ultra violet rays under this license is substantially harmful to the user of such milk, or to the milk itself, the licensee shall have the right to cancel this license."

In a memorandum dated February 8, 1939, Dr. Russell described a similar position of the Foundation in regard to high dosages of Vitamin D: "Steenbock is of the opinion that in view of the fact that Vitamin D is no longer a distinctive Steenbock product but can be secured from a variety of sources that the Foundation might as well favor the commercialization of high dosages unless there is *very* serious objection on the part of the A.M.A. officials toward a move of this sort."

It is to be noted that in neither of these cases is the Foundation concerned with public benefit or medical approval, but only with *substantial harm* and a *very serious medical objection.*

Another instance of the Foundation's regard for the public interest is the Snider Packing Company matter. In 1931 the Snider Packing Company obtained irradiated yeast from Fleischman to add to Snider's tomato juice. The results were apparently not too satisfactory. After this 1931 failure, Snider was persuaded to continue the license and the Foundation undertook to supervise the activation of the tomato juice. Steenbock and Scott recommended Acetol irradiated ergosterol and this recommendation was followed.

Despite the recommendations and supervision and guarantees of the Foundation, the Vitamin D content of the Snider tomato juice did not come up to expectations. This inadequacy was known to Snider, Acetol, and the Foundation, and on February 27, 1933, Russell wrote to Acetol stating:

"It would be most unfortunate if any publicity was to occur as a result of the reduced potency of the Snider product and it would not only ruin the Snider business in this product, but would affect most disastrously you as well as ourselves. If the Government were to discover this situation and publish the result, it would do irreparable injury to the whole Vitamin D situation in foods."

The correspondence does not show whether any of the Snider products reached the market under false labels, but the Foundation's concern in the matter is clear. The Foundation feared only publicity or discovery by the Government.

In 1934 and 1935 some research workers, and especially Dr. Reed of the University of Illinois, found that large doses of Vitamin D were highly beneficial in severe cases of asthma, hayfever and arthritis. These large doses required a highly concentrated product which was most easily used in the form of gelatin capsules. The Foundation and its licensees were greatly interested in this project, but feared the effect this concentrate might have on the pricing structure of viosterol. These fears and a suggested solution are referred to in a report of a conference between Russell and Ross of the Foundation and

Nielsen of Abbott, held early in February 1935. This report, signed by Nielsen, states:

"Mr. Nielsen stated that if the capsules were priced considerably lower than the commercial product unit for unit, nothing would prevent the hospitals from opening the capsules and diluting the content with vegetable oil to obtain a '250D' solution far below the regular cost.

"Dean Russell asked for suggestions to prevent this. Mr. Nielsen stated that Abbott Laboratories would give further thought to this problem. Tentatively, he suggested that the concentrate might be denatured by the addition of a drug also indicated in these cases—Ephedrine, for example—that the product be considered as a drug, not a vitamin, and that it be distributed for clinical trial under a special name—all provided that the licensees agree. *Any untoward effects from it thus would not reflect on the Viosterol products on the market.*"

Despite its lofty objectives, the licensing program of the Foundation appears to have resulted actually in a substantial reduction of research and development. Its attitude toward research is indicated in a letter from Russell to the licensees dated August 24, 1936:

"We are hardly interested in the prosecution of problems of a purely scientific character that come to us from outside institutions. Nevertheless, if this is a problem that has definite commercial possibilities, we should not make a hasty adverse decision."

In a letter dated January 6, 1937, addressed to Elley of duPont, Waddell of duPont referred to a meeting in Madison with members of the Foundation and stated:

"He [Steenbock] mentioned that most of the pharmaceutical licensees had not been interested in obtaining rights to the manufacture of crystalline Vitamin D (from ergosterol) and that the present situation might find them in the same attitude. He admitted, however, that if the patent situation and licensing arrangements worked out so that the five pharmaceutical companies were again in a position of having an exclusive hold on the synthetic Vitamin D field that undoubtedly they would be very much interested."

Thus, in spite of the acknowledged superiority of one form of Vitamin D, the Foundation was reluctant to do any research whatever unless the willingness and cooperation of the licensees showed a definite promise of substantial profits.

The effect of the licensing policy on the research activities of licensees is explained in a letter from Kupperian of Acetol to Waddell, research director of Acetol. This letter states:

"According to my reading of the contract with Wisconsin Alumni Research Foundation, we are not at liberty to use yeast in connection with irradiated ergosterol, this field being reserved exclusively to Fleischmann. In view of this fact, I think we ought not to waste time and money on experiments in connection with yeast."

In at least one case where the Foundation sponsored and financed research, the publication of the results of the research were suppressed by the Foundation because they were at variance with the Foundation's commercial interests. In an attempt to eliminate the non-infringing product of General Mills from competition with the Viosterol of the pharmaceutical licensees, the Foundation attempted to prove that Viosterol was clinically superior to the General Mills product. To accomplish this, the Foundation made a grant to Drs. Smith and Owens of Freedmen's Hospital in Washington, D. C., to run certain tests comparing the effectiveness of the General Mills product and Viosterol, and to prepare an article for the medical journals on the results. On June 17, 1936, Drs. Smith and Owens submitted to the Foundation their article, which contains the following conclusion:

"A comparative study of nine cases of varying degrees of rickets receiving 800 U.S.P. units of Squibb's Viosterol daily with eleven comparable cases receiving 800 U.S.P. units of American Pharmaceutical Company Viosterol [General Mills' product] shows no significant difference in rate or degree of healing as determined (1) by X-ray of the wrists and (3) Ca and P determination on the blood."

The attitude of the Foundation and its licensees to this article is described in a letter from Lescohier of Parke-Davis to Anderson of Squibb, dated July 6, 1936:

"If this article is published the Steenbock group are certainly in the position of being hung with their own rope. I should like to see the publication suppressed but am pretty certain that Meade Johnson will see that it is published since they are no longer vitally interested in Viosterol. Certainly anything that can be done to delay publication would be advisable."

In a letter dated August 17, 1936, Scott of the Foundation expressed the Foundation's attitude on this article as follows:

"From the outset, of course, we have been opposed to publication of this paper in any form. We have advised Dr. Smith that it was necessary to get the opinions of the pharmaceutical committee, and we intend to confer with them in the near future advising them that publication of the work is not desirable."

The Foundation has also suppressed the use of competing patents. Article II of the Supplemental Agreement of June 3, 1937, between the Foundation and Meade Johnson, Squibb, Parke-Davis, and Abbott provides for the licensing of additional pharmaceutical manufacturers who had been using Sperti Patent No. 1,676,579 on the irradiation of pharmaceutical products. This section provides:

"It is understood and agreed that such additional Licensees shall be prohibited, by appropriate restrictions in any license agreements that may be entered into between the Licensor and such additional Licensees, from employing the process described and claimed in United States Letters Patent No. 1,676,579 to George Sperti and from advertising the use of said process in connection with products sold under said license agreements. . ."

Thus, the results of the Foundation's licensing program have been to stifle its own research activities and the research activities of its licensees, to prevent the publication of information which might jeopardize the Foundation's financial interests, and to suppress competing patents. Certainly, these are peculiar results of a program instituted "to protect the public" and "to prevent unscrupulous commercialism."

One of the most important fields in the Foundation's scheme of exploitation is the pharmaceutical field. All Vitamin D products used in the treatment or prevention of human ills are embraced within the pharmaceutical field, and restrictions in this field thus have a direct and immediate effect on the health and well-being of the general public. Also, at the time the Foundation embarked on its licensing program, the pharmaceutical field probably was one of the most promising, both from a publicity and a profit standpoint.

In or about March 1929, the Foundation made agreements with five licensees, all manufacturers of pharmaceuticals: Meade Johnson & Co., Winthrop Chemical Company, Abbott Laboratories, Parke-Davis & Company, and E. R. Squibb & Sons. These agreements have been amended several times by letter agreements and supplemental agreements. Two letters, dated March 20, 1939 and April 27, 1939, offer the licensees certain royalty reductions, and it is assumed that these reductions were accepted. These letters do not, however, make any substantial changes in the restrictive provisions of the agreement.

This combination in restraint of trade between the Foundation and its licensees is expressed in various ways throughout the pharmaceutical licenses. For example, Article XII of the agreement of March 21, 1929, fixed minimum prices for the sale of irradiated pharmaceutical products. This article contains the following language: "Such prices so established shall remain in effect indefinitely but may be changed by the Licensor not less than ninety (90) days after consultation with all of the Licensees of this group."

Article XIII of the agreement of March 21, 1939, states that the potencies of the pharmaceutical products shall remain fixed "until and unless changed by the mutual understanding of a majority of the licensees of this group." Article XVII prevents the assignment of the licenses "without the written consent of the Licensor, the Patentee and the Licensees under similar licenses." Each of the agreements with Abbott, Meade Johnson, Squibb and Parke-Davis, executed June 3, 1937, also contains long recitals regarding the provisions to be introduced into a new contract with Winthrop Chemical Co., Inc.

Price stabilization was one of the main considerations offered by the Foundation to its licensees in exchange for the royalties. It might almost be said that this price stabilization was the bait which made the licensing scheme of the Foundation so attractive to the various manufacturers. Clough of Abbott wrote to Russell of the Foundation on April 21, 1936, and referred to the importance of price-fixing activities of the Foundation as follows: "It was argued by your Trustees that under our arrangement with the Foundation, we were given certain benefits of price stabilization which was well worth the additional *5%*."

That price-fixing was one of the most important points in the pharmaceutical licensing plan is demonstrated by a memorandum of a conference between Anderson and Lewis of Squibb and Ross and Barney of the Foundation on February 23, 1939:

"We outlined the high potency D situation both with respect to Merrell and Winthrop. Their reaction was first that Squibb would have no objection to Merrell's continuing to sell its concentrated viosterol if we could line up Merrell on its regular viosterol from the standpoint of container size and price. We indicated that this latter could be accomplished."

Further, the papers indicate that this price-fixing was carried over into the field of resale prices. This is brought out in a letter from R. D. Keim of Squibb to Dean Russell of the Foundation dated July 23, 1934:

"We gave this matter our very serious consideration and wrote to all the licensees, under date of July 19, 1934, as per copy enclosed and we firmly believe that our suggested *Full Retail Prices per package to the consumer and Minimum Retail Prices per package to the consumer* for Viosterol in Oil and Cod Liver Oil with Viosterol are more in line with present market trends and the present economic market conditions than those proposed by Parke-Davis & Company.

"We are desirous of acting in harmony with all the other licensees of the Wisconsin Alumni Research Foundation in regard to the stabilization of the market for Viosterol in Oil and Cod Liver Oil with Viosterol. However, we firmly believe that it is necessary to establish a schedule of Minimum Retail Prices to the consumer such as we have suggested in order to bring about such stabilization."

Prices were not only fixed; they were fixed arbitrarily at levels which can only be regarded as extortionate in view of the economic status of the people whose need for Vitamin D was the greatest. (Barney, the business manager of the Foundation, once stated on examination in a lawsuit: "It is my understanding that rickets is found to a great extent in the so-called poorer class of people.") Despite this full awareness of the incidence of their high price policy, the Foundation and its licensees remorselessly maintained prices on the Viosterol products so high that their use was practically restricted to those who had least need for them. This is recognized in a letter dated March 30, 1934, from Russell to the pharmaceutical licensees: "Very severe criticism from certain prominent pediatricians has been lodged against the Foundation on account of the alleged high retail prices of certain Vitamin D preparations."

The price-fixing activities of the Foundation also extended to sales to Federal, State and local governments and government agencies. On May 10, 1940, W. S. Merrell Company wrote to the Foundation:

"We have an inquiry from the Government for a substantial quantity of Irradiated Ergosterol and are wondering if we shal have to abide by the price schedule in our license agreement ir quoting. In other words, would our quotation have to be th same as our minimum price to wholesalers, or could we figur on a reasonable profit basis taking our cost on such a large quan tity for one shipment into consideration?"

The letter also contained a postscript: "We know that th price would have to be much lower than our price to the whole salers to secure the order." In spite of the fact that Merre was merely asking to quote on a "reasonable profit basis" an assured the Foundation that the price would have to be "muc lower . . . to secure the order," the business manager of Found tion replied on May 13, 1940:

"Under the present license agreement with your compar and the other pharmaceutical licensees of the Foundation und the Steenbock patents, the minimum price to be quoted to government institutions is the minimum wholesale price as outlined in your contract, less two per cent discount for cash if paid by the tenth of the following month.

"All of the other pharmaceutical licenses of the Foundation have operated under this arrangement for some time. We note, however, your postscript which indicates that the quotation to the government will have to be lower than the price to wholesalers in order to secure the order. We dislike to see your company or any of our other licensees lose business."

The pharmaceutical agreements fix both the potency and the quantities in which Vitamin D concentrates may be sold by the pharmaceutical licensees. The purpose and effect of these additional controls were stated by an official of the Foundation. "We feel that it is perfectly proper to control the price of Viosterol and cod liver oil from a legal standpoint and, unless we control the potency of the product and size of the container, price control of the product, of course, would be rather useless."

The pharmaceutical agreements specified that potencies could be changed only by "mutual agreement of Licensees of this group," while container sizes could be changed by "mutual understanding of a majority of the Licensees of this group." Operations were in exact accord with these provisions, and only unanimous approval by the licensees could authorize potency changes. Notes of a phone conversation of March 30, 1932, between Nielsen of Meade Johnson and Russell of the Foundation state: "Russell said under no condition could such approval be given. That Meade Johnson had no warrant in changing the potency without the knowledge and approval and consent, not only of the Foundation but also of the other four licensees."

Prior to December 24, 1936, the Foundation and its pharmaceutical licensees maintained a very effective black list and white list of dealers. While the approval of dealers was ostensibly within the exclusive control of the Foundation, actually it was again a matter for vote by the licensees. L. D. Barney, business manager of the Foundation, described the program to Dr. Russell, director of the Foundation, in a memorandum dated November 6, 1935:

"As you know, the usual procedure in handling requests of wholesale drug concerns with respect to their addition to the approved wholesale list for the sale of Viosterol products is for the Foundation to send the name and address of this company to the five licensees. They, in turn, investigate the company and report back to whether or not they favor the addition of the said company to the list. The general procedure set up several years ago was that a majority of the licensees (three) would constitute sufficient authority on the part of the Foundation to add the name of the company to the approved list.

"By reason of the manner in which these are handled, it is impossible for us to tell the licensee when we refuse their request anything other than the fact that the Committee, which handles the request, did not approve their application, or, stated in another way, the Committee voted in the negative. Obviously, we cannot say that our licensees did not favor the addition of this company to the group."

W. N. Larson of Meade Johnson recognized that this black list and white list might be illegal, and referred to it in a letter dated December 22, 1936, to Ward Ross, Counsel for the Foundation. He sent copies to each of the other pharmaceutical licensees. Larson's letter states:

"We would have no objection to the Foundation acting as a clearing house for information relative to those to whom wholesale terms on Viosterol and Cod Liver Oil with Viosterol are extended, except we wonder if such action might not be construed as a violation of law. Anyone investigating this activity might well inquire as to why this was done, if some action which could be construed as collusion or restraint of trade were not contemplated."

One of the principal functions of the black listing and white listing of wholesalers and retailers was the maintenance of resale prices. This is explained in a letter dated June 29, 1931, from W. N. Larson of Meade Johnson to N. A. Buttle of Winthrop, with copies to the other licensees and to the Foundation. This letter states:

"To our knowledge there have been very few departures from the suggested minimum price, and these departures have been confined to a very few relatively unimportant wholesale druggists whose objectives unlike ours, are not to stabilize conditions in the drug trade. It is the legal right of any manufacturer to refuse to sell to a wholesaler or any other customer in fact, who will not carry out his wishes. I hope that it will not be necessary, but it is entirely possible that it may become desirable for the Foundation to make the list of preferred jobbers a trifle more exclusive than it is at the present time. We would work with the Foundation in any reasonable steps in that direction. Better proof of our desire to have this matter straightened out could hardly be given, we believe."

At least as early as 1933, the Foundation and the pharmaceutical licensees realized that this black list was illegal. On May 11, 1933, Larson of Meade Johnson wrote to Gunn, attorney for the Foundation, regarding this black list:

"Licensees cannot make agreements among themselves in these matters and must, of course, take the position that they are acting under instructions from the Wisconsin Alumni Research Foundation. The revelation that that is not the case might prove to be very embarrassing, as you probably realize.

My suggestion is that, in cases of this kind, you simply inform the inquiring party that your action was guided by a committee, operating under the Wisconsin Alumni Research Foundation, and that this committee does not reveal its reasons for taking any action of this kind."

Probably in part on account of this growing disquietude concerning the lawfulness of their undercover boycott, in part also, perhaps, because of the vast amount of detail work involved in maintaining the list, the Foundation ceased rendering this service for its licensees some time late in 1936. On December 24, 1936, the business manager of the Foundation referred a prospective wholesaler to the pharmaceutical licensees for direct action.

The pharmaceutical agreements were thus far more than mere restrictive patent licenses. Prices, potencies, dosages and container sizes were fixed by the licensees jointly and black lists of price-cutting dealers were established and maintained. The Foundation offered little more than a facade of respectability to conceal these activities, and it was for this concealment that the licensees were willing to pay so handsomely.

The remaining agreements of the Foundation prohibit the other licensees from invading the pharmaceutical field. Several of the agreements prohibit, in express terms, sales of activated products for pharmaceutical uses, others so limit the potency of the licensed product as to make it worthless for medicinal purposes, while still others merely limit the right of the licensee to claim curative properties for his product in his advertising.

All the agreements of the Foundation clearly show the intention to protect the exclusive market of the pharmaceutical licensees in the human medicine field. Actually this practice is carried to a ridiculous extent. The following statement appears in a memo note of November 14, 1935, written by Ward Ross,

General Counsel for the Foundation, regarding a conference with Dr. Hooper of Winthrop:

"With regard to the comparison between Viosterol and Drisdol, I asked Hooper how he would like it if our milk licensees said that one quart of irradiated milk was equal to 10 drops of Viosterol. Hooper claimed that this would be an invasion of the pharmaceutical field by our milk licensees and that they would be selling milk as medicine."

Apparently, the licensees are prevented from telling the truthful merits of their products if the truth would cause an overlapping of the artificial division of fields.

Another industry capable of using large quantities of Vitamin D was the bread industry. Under an agreement dated November 15, 1939, this field is allocated exclusively to duPont. DuPont's chief concern in the bread field was price "stabilization" which to duPont meant the maintenance of high price levels. DuPont was even willing to share the field with Standard Brands to accomplish this end. A memorandum, dated September 19, 1935, from Mr. Kenneth T. King of duPont to Mr. Ralph Horton and Mr. W. S. Kies, a Trustee of the Foundation, states: "We would be willing for the Foundation to grant non-exclusive license for the sale of Vitamin D from Ergosterol in the bread field to the Fleischmann Company, providing the price of Vitamin D in the bread field shall be stabilized." The agreement between duPont and the Foundation expressly stipulates the limits of licensees' discretion in price policy. Article 2 (C) provides: "DuPont shall not sell said irradiated or activated Ergosterol or its derivatives at a higher price than one dollar and a half ($1.50) or a lower price than ninety-five cents ($.95) per million U.S.P.A. (revised 1934) Vitamin D Units.

The Foundation's support of duPont's policy of high prices

is indicated in a letter dated July 18, 1935, from Barney to Atkins of duPont which states: "Dr. Waddell stated that it was his opinion that if General Baking came back into the picture a higher price for ergosterol should be charged. We discussed the possibility of a price of $1.25 to $1.50 per million Steenbock units."

So long as the Foundation could be "merciless in beating out competition" price-fixing at these levels was quite attractive. But by 1940 the weakness of the Steenbock patents was so apparent that the fixed prices became a competitive hazard. On March 5, 1940, King of duPont wrote to the business manager of the Foundation:

"In reply to your letter of February 24th we are very much interested in modifying our contract with respect to the maximum and minimum provisions in the baking field. In fact, we believe the simplest way to handle this question is to delete from our present contract the clause specifying maximum and minimum provisions. This, of course, was explained to you over the telephone in our recent conversation concerning General Baking. I believe unless some change is made in the maximum and minimum provisions all business in this field will be lost by the licensees of the Foundation."

The Foundation recognized the need for abandoning these artificially high price levels and on March 14, 1940, Barney of the Foundation wrote to King of duPont referring to "a quotation from General Mills at a price of 60c per million" and stated: "This will acknowledge receipt of your letter of March 5th regarding the maximum and minimum price provisions with respect to the baking field. Shortly, Ward [Ross of the Foundation] will send Art [Connolly of duPont] either a letter agreement or supplemental contract deleting this provision from the contract." On July 19, 1940, Connolly wrote Ross again asking elimination of the price-fixing provision and finally on July 30, 1940, Ross of the Foundation wrote to duPont deleting the price-fixing paragraph from Article 2 (C) of the agreement.

DuPont's aim in all of its Vitamin D operations was to obtain high, non-competitive prices for its products. This thought is expressed time and time again. A memorandum dated July 26, 1932, from Bradshaw to Atkins, both of Acetol, states: "This morning I reported to Mr. Protto and Mr. Robinson regarding conversation with Dean Russell and also the known facts concerning Lever Bros. business. It was Mr. Protto's feeling that we should raise our prices as much as possible and not sell the material cheap." The next day Atkins replied:

"It seems obvious to me that we should always try to get the maximum price for any of our goods, keeping in mind the possible potential volume and competitive conditions.

"According to authentic price information which we have secured, Fleischmann have been selling and offering Vitamin D at slightly less than $1.00 per 1,000,000 Steenbock Rat Units. This is what influenced my suggested price of $1.00 to Lever Brothers and I was very much surprised when you informed me that Fleischmann was not in a position to furnish irradiated ergosterol. If this were true, I apparently had gone too low on our initial price in view of the fact that we were the exclusive source of supply."

The profit levels resulting from the Foundation's activities were enormous. In a letter dated March 9, 1938, addressed to Ward Ross of the Foundation, King of duPont stated: "With respect to the Chesney matter, all I know is that 35c per million units was quoted to General Baking Company."

Vitamin D is of the greatest importance to expectant and nursing mothers, infants, and children and, consequently, milk is one of the most natural and most important vehicles for this vitamin. The Council on Foods of the American Medical Association stated in the *Journal of the American Medical Association* for January 16, 1937, "Of all the common foods available, milk is most suitable as a carrier of added Vitamin D. Vitamin D is concerned with the utilization of calcium and phosphorous of which milk is an excellent source." Next to the pharmaceutical industry, milk was probably the most promising outlet for Vitamin D from a profit standpoint. The Foundation therefore became active in promoting the use of Vitamin D in the milk industry.

On November 1, 1938, the Foundation granted licenses to five producers of evaporated milk, The Borden Company, Carnation Company, Indiana Condensed Milk Company, Nestle's Milk Products, Inc., and Pet Milk Company, to activate evaporated milk. The agreements allocate the evaporated milk field exclusively to these five producers. Like the Foundation's other agreements, these evaporated milk agreements provide for the maintenance of the division of fields. Article XX, in protecting the evaporated milk field, states: "The Licensor agrees that in all licenses for the activation of fluid milk by the use of irradiated ergosterol or by direct application of ultra violet rays, it will incorporate a provision preventing the use or sale of such activated milk by such licensees for the manufacture of activated unsweetened evaporated milk."

The rights of the evaporated milk producers were similarly restricted to prevent encroachment on other exclusive fields. Article XII specifically protects the pharmaceutical field by providing that "said evaporated milk shall not be intended or sold as a cure for rickets." The other fields of use of Vitamin D are protected from invasion by activated evaporated milk by Article IX which provides: "The Licensee agrees that it will not knowingly directly or indirectly sell its unsweetened evaporated milk activated under this license to others . . . as a source of Vitamin D for any other product when such product is intended to be sold or resold on a commercial basis."

There are several methods by which fluid milk may be activated and the Foundation has issued licenses for each of these methods. In one method, irradiated yeast is fed to cows to increase the Vitamin D content of the milk; in the second method, the milk is irradiated directly; and in the third method, an activated concentrate is introduced into the milk.

The Bill of Particulars in the Vitamin Technologists suit lists 138 dairies licensed to activate milk by feeding irradiated yeast to cows. In its agreement with West Haven Creamery, Inc., which is typical of all of the licensees of this class, the Foundation licensed and empowered the licensee to purchase from Standard Brands, Incorporated, dried yeast "antirachitically activated" upon the following terms and conditions:

"First: The Licensee shall buy and use such yeast for no other purpose than that of feeding cows to impart antirachitic qualities to milk.

. . . . .

"Fourth: The Licensee shall not sell any of its antirachitically activated milk to others for use or incorporation in any other marketed product when Vitamin D or antirachitic claims are made or intended to be made for such other marketed product.

"Fifth: The activated yeast purchased by Licensee pursuant to this License shall not be resold or otherwise used except for feeding the same to the Licensee's animals, pursuant to the conditions of this license."

The Steenbock patents do not even purport to cover anything more than a process of irradiating or an irradiated product. Under no circumstances could the milk from an irradiated-yeast-fed cow be an infringement of the Steenbock patents. Article Fourth is a bare-faced attempt to carry out the artificial division of fields. Milk from an irradiated-yeast-fed cow could, for example, be used in the commercial making of bread, but such use would be an invasion of the exclusive bread and bread-stuffs field. It was, therefore, necessary for the Foundation to insert this limitation in the West Haven Creamery's license even though the limitation was entirely outside the Steenbock patents.

The prohibition of resale in Article Fifth likewise lacks any taint of legal justification. A patentee's right under a patent is completely exhausted by the first sale of the patented product. Here again the Foundation is seeking to prevent any use of the irradiated yeast which may in any way conflict with the division of fields.

As the demand for activated milk increased, the addition of concentrates was accepted by the medical profession. This business was so attractive that the Foundation decided to engage in the sale of these concentrates for addition to milk. The Foundation did not, however, wish to enter a market in which any competition existed and since Standard Brands had rights in this field, it was essential that the Standard Brands competition be eliminated. In the agreement of February 1, 1939, the Foundation agreed to pay Standard Brands 40% of the profits derived by the Foundation from the sale of concentrates in return for Standard Brands' withdrawal and agreement not to, compete.

Vitamin D is of the utmost importance in the poultry industry since it is essential for the prevention and cure of rickets and for bone development, egg production and hatchability. Prior to the war some Vitamin D could be obtained from cod and other fish liver oils, but at the present time, the requirements must be obtained almost exclusively from synthetic Vitamin D. Even apart from war time shortages, synthetic Vitamin D presents certain advantages over fish liver oils. The synthetic product may be used for forced feeding without adversely affecting the flavor of the poultry, while too generous use of fish liver oils results in a somewhat fishy flavor.

The size of the poultry market in the United States involves almost astronomical figures. The crop report of September 1, 1943 of the United States Department of Agriculture on poultry and egg production states that there were over 316,000,000 laying hens; over 318,000,000 pullets and over 224,000,000 chicks. The egg production for August 1943 was 3,863,000,000. This crop report also states that the average cost of feed for farm poultry ration on August 15, 1943 was $2.13 per hundred pounds. Dr. Harry Titus of the Poultry Nutrition Section of the Bureau of Animal Industries of the Department of Agriculture estimates that 25,000,000 tons of commercial mixed feed are used annually in the poultry industry and that 75% of this feed is fortified with Vitamin D.

The wartime demands on meat make the poultry market unusually important and any artificial restraints or artificial price levels affecting the poultry market are of the most serious national importance.

The discovery upon which Steenbock's patent No. 1680818 is based is that certain substances, known as pro-vitamins take on antirachitic properties when irradiated with ultra violet light. These pro-vitamins are sterols which may be obtained from either vegetable or animal sources and the effectiveness of the irradiated product is dependent upon the nature of the pro-vitamin.

In the early days, vegetable pro-vitamins were used almost exclusively but it was subsequently found that the animal pro-vitamins were superior. Vegetable pro-vitamins were unsuitable for poultry feeding and the exploitation of this market awaited the development of the animal pro-vitamins, cholesterol and 7-dehydrocholesterol.

The animal and poultry feed field had been exclusively allocated to duPont and its predecessor, Acetol. This exclusive arrangement highlights the artificial nature of the Foundation's division of fields. In the case of cows Vitamin D in the feed will result in a Vitamin D content in the milk. Vitamin D may also have some antirachitic effect on the cow itself. In interpreting this provision of its agreement with the Foundation, duPont was obliged to consider the question whether the effect of the Vitamin D feed is in the cow or in the milk. Finally, however, duPont resolved the doubt in its own favor. A letter dated February 20, 1935, addressed to Kupperian of duPont, from Connolly, a duPont attorney, states: "Irradiated cholesterol may therefore be used in feed for cows regardless of whether its purpose is to enhance the Vitamin D content of the milk or prevent rickets in the cow itself."

Prior to 1936, duPont recognized the importance of the animal sterols, cholesterol and 7-dehydrocholesterol, in the poultry feed field. DuPont immediately set out to secure a monopoly over these pro-vitamins and through them to control the entire poultry feed field. The first step in this direction is described in a letter dated January 21, 1936 from King of duPont to Nielsen of Abbott which states:

"We were, of course, largely interested in the poultry field, and to protect our position had made tentative arrangements to secure all of the available cholesterol in the country, or perhaps we might say, in the world."

Apart from attempting to corner the sources of animal sterols, duPont also sought exclusive rights in the field of animal sterols within the licensing scheme of the Foundation. The agreement of November 15, 1935 between the Foundation and duPont grants duPont an exclusive license to irradiate sterols from animal sources. When the Foundation wished to grant new licenses and submitted the proposed licenses to duPont for approval, duPont insisted upon retaining exclusive rights in the animal pro-vitamin field. In a report to the Executive Committee of duPont recommending approval of the Foundation's license to Merrell, E. G. Robinson states:

"The Foundation now wishes to grant a license to the William S. Merrell Company of Cincinnati, Ohio, limited to Vitamin D from non-animal sources for sale only as medicinals or pharmaceuticals for human use, which this department is willing to approve. It is limited to non-animal sources in the pharmaceutical field and, therefore, we do not think it will materially interfere with our own developments. Also, the Foundation is able to grant a license with respect to yeast ergosterol without our permission, since that product is not in our license field; and if the license to Merrell is limited to yeast we will not have the opportunity of selling Merrell our own ergosterol."

Thus, while duPont desired to protect its animal sterol field it did not wish the Merrell license so limited as to deprive duPont of a potential market for non-yeast ergosterol. In both instances the Foundation was most willing to cooperate.

8

Quebracho Extract

Quebracho extract is of great use to the nation in the war effort. It is a material which has been found most desirable for tanning the leather which goes into the shoes, harness, straps and other leather articles of the armed forces. It is of some interest to every man, woman and child whose ration stamps are used to buy a pair of shoes.

Practically all heavy leather tanned in this country has been tanned by use of a blend in which this material is an important ingredient. It comes from the southern part of South America, and there have been times when it was difficult, and others when it appeared it might be impossible, to ship the material to this country. The production and sale of the material is controlled by a monopoly pool or cartel, and this country is at the mercy of the pool in procuring the material in adequate quantities and at a reasonable price. The pool has exercised its power to curtail the quantity shipped to this country, to prevent any adequate stock pile in this country, and to raise prices out of proportion to any increase in costs.

In the Spring of 1942 the Department of Justice submitted the facts of this monopoly pool to a Federal Grand Jury in

New York, and it promptly returned an indictment against five American corporations, one Canadian and one British corporation, and five individuals, officials of four of the American corporations. Pleas of *nolo contendere* were subsequently entered by three of the American corporations and four of their officials. Fines were levied against and paid by these defendants, totalling $59,002. A *nolle prosequi* was entered as to the two remaining American corporations, the two British corporations, and one official. The reason for the *nolle prosequi* in the case of the two foreign corporations was that they were outside the jurisdiction of the court.

The national interest in such a situation plainly warranted a diligent effort long ago to find an adequate substitute which would relieve us from entire dependence upon the ability and willingness of a foreign cartel to supply us with a vital material.

The extract is obtained from the quebracho tree. For commercial purposes the growth of these trees is limited to Argentina and Paraguay. Although there are quebracho forests in southern Brazil, the extract manufactured from these trees is inferior to Argentine and Paraguayan extract, and cannot compete favorably with it in the market. Ninety-eight per cent of the world production of quebracho wood and extract comes from Argentina and Paraguay. In 1942 the total production amounted to approximately 300,000 metric tons of extract and was valued at $25,000,000.

This war has naturally affected the market for quebracho in Europe. Several years before the war the German Government took steps to render that country less dependent upon the continuance of quebracho imports. Clauses were inserted in all Army and Navy contracts for the purchase of leather goods that at least 12 per cent of such goods should be tanned by German-manufactured tanning agents. This resulted in the development of a new industry based upon the production of tanning material from German trees. Tannic acid was extracted from the oak trees of South Germany and was permitted to find a place in the tanning industry by reason of the Government policy. Thus the German leather industry gradually became independent of quebracho importation from South America.

The loss of the continental European market due to the war was not felt to any great extent by the quebracho exporters because of the great increase of exports to the United States. During the war the imports of quebracho almost doubled due to the tremendous production of leather goods for the armed forces.

The quebracho industry consists of twenty-two producers in Argentina and Paraguay. Five of these are owned or controlled by the British corporation, The Forestal Land, Timber and Railways, Ltd., through its Argentine subsidiary, La Forestal Argentina S. A. de Tierras, Maderas y Explotaciones Commerciales e Industriales. These five companies have a productive capacity which constitutes approximately 57 per cent of the total capacity.

All producers, except four having a capacity of about eleven per cent of the entire industry, are members of a Quebracho Pool which regulates the production and sale of the product. Quebracho is sold by official agents of the Pool, and it recognizes two official agents in the United States: The Tannin Corporation and the International Products Corporation, both of New York.

Forestal of England controls La Forestal of Argentina through the ownership of a majority of its stock and a substantial portion of its bonds. One John B. Sullivan, Chairman of the Board of Forestal of England, is also the manager of Forestal of Argentina. Sullivan is an Argentine citizen who was formerly a citizen of the United States and a graduate of Harvard College.

By reason of La Forestal's ownership of 57 per cent of the total productive capacity of quebracho in South America, which is approximately eight times the capacity of its next largest competitor, Forestal has completely dominated the quebracho industry. Its policy has been to restrict production and maintain high prices. Forestal's economic dominance in Argentina has enabled it to exert a great influence upon the government of Argentina. For example, in 1942 the efforts of John B. Sullivan alone were primarily responsible for the imposition by the Argentine Minister of Agriculture of highly restrictive export quotas upon each producer. These restrictions were imposed upon the industry at a time when it appeared that the efforts of Forestal to continue similar restrictions upon the South American producers might fail.

Forestal's domination extends not only over the production of quebracho, but over its distribution as well, including importation into this country. Through St. Helen's Ltd., a Canadian corporation, Forestal of England owns substantially all of the stock of Tannin Products Corporation, a Delaware corporation, which in turn owns all the capital stock of The Tannin Corporation, a New York corporation.

The Tannin Corporation imports approximately 70 per cent of all quebracho extract consumed in the United States. The Tannin Corporation has been controlled by Forestal of England since 1913 and during the past thirty years its controlling officials have been completely subservient to the policies of Forestal of England. Thus Forestal controls this material from the tree to the United States consumer.

The questionable character of the functioning of these American subsidiaries is indicated by portions of a letter written December 23, 1941, by Carl B. Ely, President of the Tannin Corporation, to J. B. Sullivan of Forestal, whom he addressed as "My dear Jack":

"You will recall the formation for good and practical reasons of the Tannin Products Corporation in 1925, at which time a very large dividend was paid, which procedure continued in a more or less degree during the following years, particularly in 1929 and 1934. The company, as you will see, earned $3,284,-427.28 and paid out dividends of $4,200,000.00. In other words, we declared practically $1,000,000 more during the sixteen-year period than we earned.

"Under the circumstances I have no fault to find with this, provided our principal stockholders, the Forestal Company, are aware of it and are prepared to take care of our money situation as the same arises. . .

"To come right down to the last analysis, we have been living on Government funds, which under proper business procedure should be reserved for income tax payments, but, as these payments are not due until next year, it has been possible to use this money. We owe the Government today $500,000. This money, together with your most helpful postponement of payments, has made it possible for us to have cash to pay the dividend we did. I believe that with the extra terms on future purchases of extract we will make our position stronger during the next six months, and we are trying diligently not to borrow from the banks, as in this particular case it would appear that such borrowing was done to pay dividends. This I believe would have a very bad effect on our good will and financial standing—and we enjoy today the good will and respect of the tanning industry as we never have before."

I have already pointed out that Forestal controls five of the South American producers. One of the other seventeen is the

International Products Corporation of New York. Another producer, Samuhi S. A., is controlled through ownership of a majority of its stock by two American corporations, Proctor Ellison and Howes Bros. of Massachusetts. International Products Corporation and Samuhi together have a capacity of about eight per cent of the entire industry. Both of these producers have been ineffective in preventing La Forestal from carrying out its policy of restricted output and high prices, and International Products has in the past frequently cooperated closely with La Forestal to further such a policy.

Since 1934 International Products Corporation has consulted with Tannin about the prices to be charged to quebracho extract consumers in the United States, so that the prices of both companies have been fixed, uniform and high. From May, 1934 to July, 1939, Tannin owned a substantial amount of the stock of International Products Corporation, and from May, 1934 until May, 1936, the president of Tannin, Carl B. Ely, was a member of the Board of Directors of International Products Corporation. On February 26, 1935, Ely wrote to Sullivan:

"I am giving the I.P.C. problems a lot of my time, and, as previously told you, have found that there is a lot to be done to straighten out that problem. I am working slowly so as not to upset the apple cart any more than is necessary. . .

"I am getting their sales policies straightened out and believe now there will be no more monkey business."

From 1934 to 1939 International Products Corporation was a member of the Quebracho Pool, and by reason of its designation as an official pool agent for the United States gave up its business of selling extract in England and in Asia.

American purchasers of quebracho might well wonder whether this American company was more concerned with giving them a good deal or with favoring certain foreign concerns, from the concluding paragraph of a letter from one of its officials to its President dated November 16, 1939:

"You undoubtedly know that Mr. Seldes was successful in substituting Casado extract to fill the order we had for Forestal for 535 tons of Supremo for delivery in Buenos Aires for shipment to Japan. We paid for the Casado extract with a dollar draft and have since received from Forestal the sterling representing the sale. The net result of the whole transaction represents a loss of a little more than a $1.00 per ton, which, as explained in a previous letter, is really not a loss at all, as we will use this extract to fill orders for North America which will net us a nice profit."

The production of Samuhi was so small, being about one per cent of the entire industry, that it could hardly contain any competitive threat to La Forestal. Nevertheless, our records show that for many years Forestal harassed this company by every means and sought to buy up its assets and its stock.

It is interesting to observe in what manner the quebracho extract pool operated to carry out Forestal's policy of restricted output and high prices. Before the formation of the Pool the price per pound of quebracho extract was 2½ cents. By the terms of the pool agreement a directive committee, dominated by Forestal, was empowered to fix the prices of all its members. The directive committee between November, 1934 and January, 1941, decreed six price rises, raising the basic price of quebracho extract for the whole world market from 2½ cents up to 4⅞ cents, an increase of nearly 100 per cent. Sullivan admitted in July, 1942, that at the then existing price, which prevails at present, Forestal was making a net profit of 33 per cent on every ton of quebracho it sold.

The exorbitant profits of the quebracho manufacturers were

severely criticized by the famous leading Argentine newspaper, *La Prensa*. The following excerpt was taken from a letter of May 20, 1936, written by the manager of the Buenos Aires office of the International Products Corporation to its president:

"Another matter, which has caused a lot of excitement amongst the manufacturers has been the inopportune declaration, made by the Chairman of the Forestal during the annual meeting of the shareholders, viz. that the understanding of the manufacturers was performed under the auspices of the Argentine Government, in other words, that the Argentine Government was really responsible for the agreement and that it was protecting the same. This news was reproduced all over the world and the *La Prensa*, the most important paper on the Southern Hemisphere, has seized the opportunity to denounce the huge profits made by the quebracho manufacturers, profits which in their opinion mean a loss for the Argentine Republic on account of the decrease in the export of both, Quebracho Extract and Logs. I am enclosing herewith the article, as appeared in the *La Prensa* of Monday the 18th. inst., and we would add this paper has on more than one occasion criticized the so-called 'gentlemen agreement.' Mr. Marti told me that he is at a loss to understand how the Baron made these declarations as Mr. Sullivan has always stressed the necessity of not mentioning the Argentine Government in connection with the manufacturers' agreement, a fact which can be noted in the balance sheets of the other companies, who, referring to the higher prices, explain that they are due to a better understanding in the sales policy abroad. Anyway, I hope that his faux pas will have no serious consequences."

To maintain high prices it was necessary to limit the production and the sale of quebracho in the world market. The method used to limit production under the pool agreement was to allocate a quota to each producer in accordance with his respective productive capacity. These quotas limited the amount of quebracho extract which any manufacturer could sell during a given period. Each member of the pool was compelled to make substantial contributions at regular periods to a so-called "battle fund" of the pool. These contributions were retained by the pool unless the producers adhered to the pool's regulations relating to prices and quotas, in which case a portion of each producer's contribution was refunded. So restrictive were these quota limitations that producers who desired to sell above their quotas often paid enormous prices to acquire the quota rights of other producers.

This rigid control of the market so severely limited the production of many companies that in 1941 several deserted the pool. These companies were LaChaquena S. A. and Cotan S. A. These two companies, together with International Products Corporation, Samuhi, and Weisburd & Cia. Ltda., a new concern, have been the only producers outside of the pool since 1941. Although the total productive capacity of these five companies did not exceed 12 per cent of the total industry, their threat of full production and decreased prices jeopardized its whole structure. To meet this threat, Forestal succeeded in persuading the Ministry of Agriculture in February, 1942, to impose export restrictions upon each producer which prevented exportation of more than approximately one-third of their total capacity. In addition, Forestal attempted to prevent companies outside the pool from shipping their extract to the United States.

One instance is the experience of Hammond and Carpenter Corporation, an independent importer which has sought to compete with The Tannin Corporation and International Products Corporation in the importation of quebracho. In February or March, 1942, J. A. Barkey, its Vice-President, attempted to import some extracts produced by Weisburd, an Argentine extract manufacturer, who entered the industry in 1941. He called at the offices of the Sprague Steamship Company and spoke to Mr. Bodemann of that company. Mr. Barkey later described the conference as follows:

"Mr. Bodemann retorted that it was very unlikely that our firm would be given any space for the reason that we were newcomers in the import of quebracho extract and for the further reason that the 'Pool' had supported his line during the lean years before the war and by reason of such support his line would be obliged to support the 'Pool' during the present emergency."

Similar sentiments were voiced by Mr. Horgan of the Stockard Steamship Corporation. The aid of the Buenos Aires Agency of Moore-McCormack was also previously enlisted. In October, 1941, the Moore-McCormack line stated that "at the request of the Forestal Company they had promised their cooperation for the purpose of keeping out any of the new brands. . . . The understanding was that whenever they were offered outside extract and they had space they were to reject it and advise the other manufacturers, who would try to offer replacement."

Forestal's tactics are well illustrated by the case of Mr. T. Valentine, exporter and concessionnaire of a projected new company. International Products Corporation was informed in September, 1941:

"[It] has proved impossible so far to reach a satisfactory agreement with the new factory at Santiago del Estero. For this reason, the Forestal Company, in an endeavor to impede the exportation of the extract, has seen all the steamship companies requesting them not to give space to any outsiders, but to advise the Forestal who would immediately offer replacement cargo. The steamship companies promised to act accordingly."

The Basal Agency had obtained shipping space for Valentine in the past. "The Basal Agency," an official of International Products wrote to Feeney a week later, "has informed us that Valentine wants to book a further 200 tons on the next steamer but that they would refuse to take it if we or the Forestal would offer them replacement cargo."

The effect of the restrictive government decrees and other measures taken by Forestal has been to force one independent, Cotan, S.A., back into the Pool, while another, Samuhi, S.A., is contemplating rejoining the Pool. It appears inevitable that within a short period of time the remaining independents will be forced into full cooperation with the Pool and that the industry's policy of restrictive production and high prices will continue unless some completely satisfactory substitute may be found for quebracho extract. Apparently the tanners in this country find that wattle extract is the only tanning product interchangeable with quebracho extract, and it is therefore significant to observe that the wattle extract industry, which is located in South and East Africa, is also controlled by Forestal of England, and that the principal importers of wattle in the United States are the Tannin Corporation and International Products Corporation.

The chief official of one of the companies which stood up against the bulldozing tactics of the Pool wrote a letter to American Tanners Ltd., on February 7, 1935. After discussing in a critical manner the actions of the Pool and referring to a conversation with an individual whom he said could be "interpreted as a stool pigeon for Forestal," he wrote:

"We also pointed out the fact that if the arbitrary methods of the gentlemen [the Pool] were pursued, that they were throwing away their markets, they were encouraging the fields of research and that they would wake up one day and find that the volume of consumption of Quebracho Extract had been greatly reduced due to the introduction of other materials which supplanted Quebracho and I cited the instance of what the tanners went through with substituted leather and how the volume of the market had never been regained and that the same thing would happen to Quebracho."

9
Titanium

The titanium industry is controlled by a typical cartel. That it is a cartel there can be no question. The president of one of the American companies which dominate it was thoughtful or thoughtless enough to define it. He wrote to one of the European officials as follows:

"May I call the proposed combination, for simplicity, a cartel? The whole purpose of the cartel is to obtain a monopoly of patents, so that no one can manufacture it [titanium] excepting the members of the cartel, and so can raise the prices by reason of such monopoly to a point that would give us much more profit on our present tonnage, but also prevent a growth in tonnage that would interfere with their greater profits in lithopone [a competing but inferior product]."

It is typical because it has utilized the devices and followed the practices which are found in greater or lesser degree in all cartel arrangements. The members of this cartel include I. G. Farbenindustrie, the German chemical trust and many other foreign companies. The American scene is dominated by three American corporations, the National Lead Company, E. I. duPont de Nemours and Co., and Titan Co., Inc. (These three companies and four of their leading officials were indicted by a grand jury in the Southern District of New York on June 28, 1943.)

The story of the titanium cartel is significant for these reasons:

1. Titanium, the most valuable and useful of all white pigments for paints, rubber products, glass, paper, enamel and other materials has been priced exorbitantly and its use restricted because of the monopolistic control exercised over it by a world-wide cartel.

2. American members of the cartel are placed in a position where they have felt obliged to help the Japanese evade the British embargo.

3. American members have seen fit to aid I. G. Farben in attempting to prevent seizure of German owned patents by the American Alien Property Custodian by the execution of specious patent assignments.

4. To attain such monopolistic control, the cartel has resorted to flagrant misuse of patents and has gone so far as to actually pay large sums to potential competitors to keep them out of the titanium business.

5. I. G. Farben, the German chemical trust, as one of the leading parties to the cartel, has dictated the terms upon which American members might do business.

6. The fact that duPont, Imperial Chemical Industries and I. G. Farben are also members of other cartels, such as that involving dyestuffs, makes their control of a fine pigment such as titanium the more objectionable.

It is difficult to think of any material which is more universally used by private citizens and by governments alike than is paint. In time of peace, the United States government buys and uses enormous quantities of paint. In this time of war its purchases account for by far the greater portion of all the paint manufactured in the entire country.

It is a fact which is not widely known that the finest of all white pigments, useful in colored paints as well as white, is titanium dioxide. It is also not generally known that titanium is the ninth most abundant element in the earth. Crude titanium is found in combination with iron in an ore called ilmenite in many places in this and other countries. It is found in purer form in the sands of Travancore Beach in India and in lesser concentration in many places.

While the element itself is abundant, no commercially practical processes for reducing it to pigment form were known until about the time of the first World War. In the relatively short period which has passed since then, technology has been developed which makes possible the manufacture of the finest pigment from titanium. It has already displaced white lead, lithopone and other pigments in a large share of the market. In hiding power (covering qualities), opacity and chemical inertness—all essential qualities for paints—titanium compounds, chiefly titanium dioxide, excel all other kinds of pigments.

Shortly after the Civil War it was discovered that titanium ore could be reduced to a powder which when mixed with oil resulted in a paint. It was not until about the beginning of World War I that a feasible method of separating titanium oxide from the ore was worked out. This was accomplished by two chemists, Dr. A. J. Rossi and L. E. Barton, whose research was done for the Titanium Alloy Manufacturing Company organized by Dr. Rossi and others in 1906. As a result of their discovery, a new corporation called the Titanium Pigment Company was formed in 1916. At that time, as well as subsequently, the leading manufacturer of white pigment was the National

Lead Company. Recognizing the implications of titanium's excellence in this field, National Lead purchased a substantial interest in the Titanium Pigment Company in 1920. The two companies continued to operate more or less separately until 1932 when National Lead acquired the entire stock of Titanium Pigment. In 1936, the latter was dissolved as a corporation and its business and properties were taken over and operated as a division of National Lead.

During substantially the same period in which this development was taking place in this country, a different process for the manufacture of titanium compounds was being developed in Norway by Gustav Jebsen. His process was patented and was exploited by a Norwegian corporation called Titan Co. A/S. At about the same time a Russian chemist named Joseph Blumenfeld was perfecting, in France, another method of manufacture, which was likewise patented. Thus prior to 1920 three groups working independently of one another had developed processes for utilizing titanium ore for production of pigments. These groups are:

1. Titanium Pigment Company, subsequently absorbed in National Lead Company.

2. Titan Co. A/S, originally organized in Norway by Jebsen for the exploitation of his developments. Eighty-seven percent of its stock was purchased by National Lead in 1927, the remaining 13% being retained by Jebsen. This company was originally intended to exploit the foreign interests of National Lead, but in 1929 National Lead and Jebson organized in Delaware a holding company called Titan Co., Inc., the sole function of which was to hold all foreign interests of the parties. Titan Co. A/S remained in existence in Norway solely as the sales agent for Titan Co., Inc.

3. The Blumenfeld Interests. Whereas National Lead and

Jebsen chose to exploit their patents by means of operating companies, Blumenfeld followed a general policy of licensing other interests.

Titanium Pigment and Titan Co. A/S entered into a contract dated July 30, 1920, which is the foundation upon which the parties and their successor companies have been able to build a cartel with monopoly ramifications extending throughout the world. This contract was to extend to 1936 and was to be automatically renewed for 10-year periods unless terminated by 5-year notice. By the terms of this agreement, National Lead (as Titanium Pigment and its successor in interest will be called) was assigned the markets of North America as its exclusive territory. Titan Co. A/S was given the rest of the world with the exception of South America which was to be common territory. The two companies granted each other exclusive licenses under their patents for their respective territories, excluding even the licensor from the licensee's territory. Each agreed not to ship into the other's territory and to prevent its licensees from shipping their finished products into the other's territory if it would interfere with the other party's sales. Any sublicensee was required to be governed by the same restrictions as the parties imposed upon themselves. The parties agreed to exchange know-how and also to permit visits of representatives to their respective plants. Each party undertook to secure from its employees assignment of any and all inventions developed by them. In acquiring rights to inventions from third parties, each agreed to secure rights for all countries within the territory of the other party.

Following the execution of the 1920 agreement, the parties operated under it until 1927.

Jebsen, having Europe as part of his territory, set up a selling company in France. This was originally intended to become a manufacturing company also, but this idea was never carried out. National Lead acquired a majority interest in this company in 1927. At the same time it acquired 87% interest in Titan Co. A/S, the Norwegian company, Jebsen retaining the remaining 13%.

Also in 1927 National Lead and Jebsen formed a new company in Germany in conjunction with I. G. Farben. This company, Titangesellschaft, G.m.b.H., was organized as part of a series of transactions including the execution of nine separate contracts. Titangesellschaft was given as its exclusive territory for manufacture and sale of titanium compounds the following countries: Germany, Russia, Austria, Hungary, Czechoslovakia, Switzerland, Rumania, Serbia, Jugoslavia, Bulgaria, Greece, Turkey, Japan, China and Spain. In 1933 Titangesellschaft eliminated potential competition on the part of the Sachtleben Company in Germany by the simple expedient of paying it a large sum of money for its agreement to stay out of the titanium business.

In 1929, National Lead and Jebsen organized in Delaware a company called Titan Co., Inc., for the purpose of holding their foreign interests. Titan Co., Inc., succeeded to the position of Titan Co. A/S (the Norwegian firm) under the basic agreement of 1920. Thus we have National Lead as successor to Titanium Pigment as one party to the basic agreement and Titan Co., Inc., owned 87% by National Lead, as the other party. However, the 1920 agreement continues in existence inasmuch as its territorial and license exchange restrictions form the basis and pattern for all the subsequent agreements. Thus, Titan Co., Inc., became entitled to all territory outside North America except as yielded up by the German agreements and others subsequent to them.

Blumenfeld transferred all his patent rights to a French

company known as Societe de Products Chemiques des Terres Rares. This concern then licensed or sold them to different companies operating in various European countries, the British Empire and United States.

In the United States, the patents were first owned by the Commercial Pigments Corporation which sold them in 1931 to the Krebs Pigment and Color Corporation. At that time, duPont owned 70% of the stock of Krebs. It subsequently acquired 100% and now operates it as the Krebs Division of duPont. National Lead entered upon negotiations with duPont looking toward an agreement which would allow the two companies to maintain a monopoly of the titanium business in this country and eliminate competition between them. I. G. Farben insisted that in any such agreement duPont must obligate itself not to compete or allow its sublicensees to compete in I. G. Farben's territory, i.e., the world outside the Western Hemisphere. When a proposed form of agreement was submitted to I. G. Farben for approval, it objected because the license given by duPont for foreign territory was a "non-exclusive license." A National Lead official reassured I. G. Farben on this score in the following language, quoted from a letter written in 1933:

"In regard to the phrase 'non-exclusive license' to which you call our attention . . . we have to refer to the United States Anti-Trust Laws which absolutely forbid the granting of exclusive licenses between two manufacturers in the United States as such a practice would tend to create a monopoly. Therefore, the use of this phrase 'non-exclusive license' is simply to comply with the United States Laws and in practice the licenses under each other's patents will undoubtedly prove to be, to all intents and purposes, exclusive."

I. G. Farben's objections having been met and other difficulties overcome, Titanium Pigments Co., Inc., and Krebs Pigment and Color Corporation, subsidiaries of National Lead and duPont, respectively, entered into an agreement dated January 1, 1933. It provided for a mutual grant of irrevocable and "non-exclusive rights" and a license within the United States to use all processes, methods and apparatus of manufacture including present and future processes and patents. It also provided that each party might sell the products resulting from the exercise of the processes in the United States, Central and South America. The territorial division of the basic agreement of 1920 was thus preserved.

The agreement also provided for the exchange of the most detailed information with respect to technical developments and know-how "to the end that all the knowledge and experience of each party in the licensed field shall be at the full disposal of the other." This provision caused some little difficulty between the parties. About 1937 Farben developed a new titanium pigment (rutile) of exceptionally fine quality which gave it a great competitive advantage. It passed the information concerning it to National Lead. The latter failed to inform duPont of this development and when duPont later discovered that such had been the case, it charged National Lead with violation of its agreement. The net result was an amendment of the agreement in 1941 by which the exchange of information provision was eliminated. Actually, duPont itself developed a similar rutile pigment and started production of it while National Lead was still guarding the secret it had received from I. G. Farben without producing the pigment.

The 1933 agreement further provided that each party was to pay a royalty to the other on the basis of titanium dioxide produced and packed by it. DuPont was to pay National Lead a royalty of 2½% based on the average published carload price, and National was to pay Krebs (duPont) 1% on a similar basis.

It was provided, however, that in no event was royalty to either party to exceed $10,000 in any given year and all royalties were to cease as of December 31, 1936. The parties undertook to employ their best efforts to acquire rights for each other from third parties and duPont further agreed to offer licenses to the foreign associates of National Lead for the various countries of the world. This virtually was a commitment by duPont to give National Lead's foreign subsidiaries a preference in granting licenses.

Following the execution of the duPont-National Lead Agreement in 1933, duPont entered into a series of four contracts with Titan Company, Inc. By these agreements, duPont agreed to turn over all its foreign patents to the various foreign associates of Titan Company, Inc. The result was a virtual consolidation of all the important titanium interests throughout the world. All commercially useful patents were under the control of the parties involved. Future control was assured by the various provisions of the agreements requiring the continuing exchange of licenses and patents to the practical exclusion of all would-be competitors.

At the time of the formation of Titangesellschaft, it was the intention of the National Lead-I. G. groups to extend their facilities into any country if and when it seemed necessary. From time to time beginning in 1933 the National-Titan-I. G. group because of threatened competition in one country after another was forced to take action to control the various competitive forces. This happened in Great Britain, Canada and Japan.

As early as 1930 the British Chemical Trust, Imperial Chemical Industries, Ltd., evidenced a desire to engage in the titanium business and in fact carried on considerable research work in that connection. This came to the attention of the National

Lead-Titan group and prompted them to take action to control the development in the British Empire. At that time, the Blumenfeld British patents were owned by National Titanium Pigments Co., Ltd. It was feared by the National Lead-Titan group that National Titanium Pigments, I. C. I. and Imperial Smelting Corporation would undertake a joint enterprise and thus offer formidable competition in that territory. After considerable negotiation, a jointly owned corporation, British Titan Products Ltd., was formed. The stock was owned 49% by Titan Co., Inc., and 51% by I. C. I., Imperial Smelting and Goodlass Wall Lead Industries, Ltd., in equal shares. In conjunction with the formation of the new corporation, the participating companies executed a series of agreements, the purpose and result of which was to divide territory and avoid competition among the various companies. The principal contract between Titan Co., Inc., and British Titan Products was to extend to 1963 and to continue in force thereafter until cancelled by either party upon twelve months' notice. It is still in effect. The Blumenfeld patents had been acquired by the British Laporte Co. and negotiations between Laporte and British Titan Products were carried on in 1940 and 1941. In August 1941 an agreement in principle was arrived at. This provided that Laporte was to receive 20% of the British market for the duration of the war. British Titan Products tried to make it for a longer period and stated its willingness to concede a larger proportion of the market, but Laporte refused. Jebsen, now as an officer of a National Lead subsidiary, gave his approval to this agreement and stated that he was quite satisfied that it was only for the duration because he felt that British Titan Products would be much better off after the war as a result of the developments which they would get from National Lead. He felt that they could use these developments to advantage in dealing with Laporte in postwar negotiations.

The most important chemical company in Canada is Canadian Industries, Ltd. (C. I. L.), most of the stock of which is owned by duPont and I. C. I. Under the basic agreement of 1920 Canada was within the territory assigned to National Lead and it supplied most of the Canadian market until the early thirties when British Titan Products was allowed to ship into Canada on a preferential basis. The British Laporte Company was also shipping into the Canadian market. Although it held the Canadian Blumenfeld patents, it did not undertake to manufacture in that country. DuPont also was exporting to Canadian buyers and for a number of years the various companies participated in price stabilizing agreements.

In 1937 National Lead and C. I. L. organized Canadian Titanium Pigments, Ltd. (51% C. I. L.—49% National Lead) for the manufacture and sale of titanium in the Canadian market. At the same time, they purchased the Blumenfeld Canadian patents from Laporte. A series of contracts executed by National Lead, C. I. L. and Canadian Titanium Pigments contain the usual provisions for division of territory, licensing of patents, control of shipment of manufactured products, exchange of know-how, etc. The principal contract extends until 1967. National Lead continues to sell Canadian Titanium Pigments all its requirements for the Canadian market. However, it is obligated to cease all exports to Canada as soon as Canadian Titanium Pigments builds a factory which is scheduled for erection immediately after the war.

The only remaining country of any commercial consequence was Japan. By virtue of the European cartel agreements, the Japanese market had been assigned to the Titangesellschaft and to the Blumenfeld French company in the ratio of 70-30. The

Titan Co., Inc., owning 50% of Titangesellschaft, profited by this arrangement. From the time of the execution of these agreements until 1937, the Japanese market was supplied with products manufactured in Germany. From time to time, however, there were indications of independent competition which finally became so threatening to their control that the National Lead-I. G. Farben interests thought it necessary to undertake development of a domestic manufacturing plant in Japan.

After considerable negotiation and the overcoming of many difficulties, the various interested companies executed a series of seven contracts providing for the formation of a new company known as Titan Kogyo Kabushiki Kaisha. The participating companies were National Lead and I. G. Farben operating through their jointly owned subsidiary, Titangesellschaft, Blumenfeld's French company, and a Japanese chemical company, the Kokusan Kogyo Kabushiki Kaisha. Neither National Lead nor Blumenfeld had any direct contact with the operations of the Japanese company inasmuch as all matters were handled through I. G. Farben by its Japanese representative, Doitsu Senryo Gomei Kaisha. By virtue of the executed contracts, Kokusan was given 50% of the stock of Titan Kogyo. Titan Co., Inc. (representing National Lead's interests) received 17½%; I. G. Farben, 17½% and Blumenfeld's French company, 15%. Because of restrictions of the German government, I. G. Farben was unable to supply capital necessary to subscribe for its share of the stock. Consequently, Titan Co., Inc., subscribed for I. G. Farben's share and gave the latter an option to purchase these shares at any subsequent time.

Because of German participation in the Japanese Titanium Company, the British Government refused to permit titanium from Travancore, India, to be exported to Japan in the fall and winter of 1940-41. Titanium was badly needed in Japan and the Japanese government had not permitted any titanium pigments to be exported for a long time. Knowing this and in spite of the fact that the situation in this country was very serious because of disruption of shipping and inadequacy of domestic supplies, nevertheless Titanium Pigment (National Lead) shipped 700 tons to Titan Kogyo Kaisha, Ltd. on March 9, 1941, thus aiding the Japanese to evade the embargo which the British had with good cause placed on sale to Japan. In a letter dated April 3, 1941, the manager of Titanium Pigments wrote to the Japanese company:

"Even at the time we made shipment to you of 700 tons on March 9th, the situation was so serious that we should have much preferred not to have released even this quantity, but in view of the fact that we had promised it to you early last fall, we felt that we should not withdraw our offer. Incidentally, at the time we made this shipment to you in March, the replacement value of that ore was more than double the price at which we invoiced it to you."

The extent to which one member of a cartel will go in protecting the interests of a foreign partner and incidentally in attempting to safeguard its own monopoly position is indicated by the following letter and resolution. The letter dated December 11, 1939, is from the manager of National Lead's Patent Department to the General Manager of the Titanium Division.

"Confirming our recent conversations, regarding exchange of title to patents, I beg to review the situation for you.

"On September 7th I wrote Dr. Jebsen, pointing out that in view of the war certain questions arose affecting the United States patents which stand in the name of Titangesellschaft and the I. G. Farbenindustrie under which we enjoy an exclusive license. We suggested to Dr. Jebsen that it might be desirable to assign to National Lead Company, in trust, the patents of the I. G. Farbenindustrie and Titangesellschaft against the possibility of the United States entering the war and taking over these patents. *The suggestion was primarily designed to protect the patent property of the I. G. Farbenindustrie and Titangesellschaft and at the same time would have protected our exclusive license by insuring that no one else could have petitioned the government to secure licenses under them.* On December 7th I received the following cable from Dr. Jebsen:

"'YOUR LETTER SEPTEMBER 7 STOP SUBJECT LEADCOS AND TITANINCS APPROVAL *HAVE AGREED ASSIGNMENT* TG PATENTS AND APPLICATIONS COUNTRIES OUTSIDE TG TERRITORY TO TITANINC AND ASSIGNMENT LEADCOS AND TITANINCS PATENTS AND APPLICATIONS COUNTRIES WITHIN TG TERRITORY TO TG STOP ASSIGNMENT PATENTS BRITISH EMPIRE FRANCE MUST BE POSTPONED DUE WAR SITUATION STOP PATENTS AND APPLICATIONS OF IG CANNOT BE INCLUDED PRESENTLY BUT QUESTION WILL BE STUDIED STOP PLEASE CABLE APPROVAL STOP GERMAN PATENTS 571387 AND 588230 AND 604311 ARE IN LEADCOS CZECHOSLOVAKIAN PATENT 39354 IN TITANIUM PIGMENT CO INCORPORATEDS NAME ALL OTHER PATENTS TG TERRITORY IN TITANINCS NAME STOP CABLE TITANINC BOARDS AUTHORISATION I ASSIGN TITANINCS PATENTS AND APPLICATIONS TO TG AS ABOVE OUTLINED STOP SUGGEST FORMAL RESOLUTION BE MADE GENERAL REGARDING ASSIGNMENT AND MAILED STOP PLEASE ACKNOWLEDGE CABLE UPON RECEIPT—JEBSEN'

"The suggestion here is that Titangesellschaft will assign their United States patents and applications to National Lead Co. and National Lead Co. and Titan Co., Inc., will assign their applications and patents in Germany, and other countries within Titangesellschaft's territory to Titangesellschaft. . . . Several years ago National Lead Company formally renounced maintenance of any European patents owned by it, putting upon Titan Co., Inc., the obligation to pay all maintenance charges and hence, under the Agreement of 1920, Titan Co., Inc., could have requested formal assignment of these patents. They have not done so in order to save the expense of preparing the assignments and recording them in the various countries. The question is, therefore, whether Titan Co., Inc., should assign its patents and applications to Titangesellschaft.

"In discussing this matter with you on December 8th, *it appeared to us that to assign these patents in Germany to Titangesellschaft might involve some risks for the future. For instance, if the Germans owned all the patents now held in Germany by Titan Co., Inc., and if, as a result of the war they were forced by their government*, or through other circumstances, *to abrogate the main agreement, they would be free to export their products and, in general, take themselves outside of the titanium family cooperation.* I cabled this thought to Dr. Jebsen, soliciting his views. A reply has just been received which reads as follows:

"'PROPOSAL MY CABLE DECEMBER 7 IS NOT TGS BUT MINE STOP CONSIDER THIS BEST PRESENT CIRCUMSTANCES TO SECURE LEGAL POSITION ALL AROUND STOP EXACTLY LEGAL POSTWAR POSITION PATENTS OTHERWISE VERY UNCERTAIN STOP *PREVENTION IMPORT PARTLY SECURED IN FUTURE BY PATENTS IN RESPECTIVE COUNTRIES BUT WILL BE CHIEFLY SECURED BY ALL COMPANIES SELFISH INTEREST IN COOPERATION BECAUSE OF ADVANTAGES ALREADY REALIZED BY EXPERIENCE.*'

"You will see that Dr. Jebsen believes that in view of the war the best possible legal position for each of the members of the family is to hold title to all patents in its territory. He believes that prevention of import and export competition will chiefly be secured in the future through the individual company's recognition of the advantages to be derived from maintaining the cooperation, having through experience appreciated the value of this cooperation.

"It should be noted in this connection that even if Titan Co., Inc., retained title to the patents in Germany, and should the government force abrogation of the main agreements, particularly with a view to fostering German exports, they will find means to negate Titan Co., Inc.'s patent rights also. *Should the situation develop where Titangesellschaft is forced, perhaps against its will, to engage in export competition with other members of the titanium family, then, as pointed out by Dr. Jebsen, that competition can be controlled by patents owned by the other members of the family in their particular territories.* Therefore, I believe we should approve Dr. Jebsen's proposal."

That this plan was put into effect is shown by a resolution adopted by the Board of Directors of Titan Co., Inc., on December 19, 1939:

"Resolved, in furtherance of that certain License Agreement between Titan Co. A/S (predecessor in interest of this corporation) and Titangesellschaft m. b. H., of Leverkusen, Germany, dated October 3/20, 1937, and pursuant to the recommendation of Dr. G. Jebsen, Vice-President of this corporation, the officers of this corporation be and they hereby are authorized and empowered to execute and deliver in its name and behalf appropriate assignments to said Titangesellschaft of all patents and patent applications of this corporation, within the Licensed Field as defined in said Agreement, in countries now embraced within the territory of said Titangesellschaft as defined in said Agreement and subsequent amendments thereto, in consideration of the execution and delivery by said Titangesellschaft to this corporation of appropriate assignments of all patents and patent applications of said Titangesellschaft, within said Licensed Field, in countries embraced within the territory of this corporation as defined in said Agreement and subsequent amendments thereto; and upon the express understanding and condition that such reciprocal assignments shall in no way alter or limit the general intent and operating effect of said Agreement of the several other rights and obligations of the respective parties thereto."

Among the patents so assigned to avoid seizure by the Alien Property Custodian is one covering the new rutile pigment previously mentioned.

In the cable which has just been cited, and the action taken pursuant to it, there is an example of postwar planning which has been all too prevalent in these cartel groups. This is not the only instance in which a German company's United States patents have been taken over by an American cartel partner to avoid seizure by the Alien Property Custodian. The understanding that such assignments shall only operate during the war and that after the war the game shall take up where it left off is of great importance. Government postwar planning should not fail to take into account and deal forcefully with the secret postwar plans of private cartels.

In a system of free enterprise, the superior product which can be produced and sold at the lowest price is able to take the place of competing products inferior in quality or higher in price. Under a cartel system inferior or more expensive products are allowed to hold a share of the market which they would lose on a competitive basis.

This is well illustrated in the case of titanium pigment and an inferior product called lithopone. The latter is a pigment in the manufacture and marketing of which duPont has taken a leading part for many years. Since 1933 National Lead and duPont have maintained identical prices for titanium compounds. There have been changes in market prices on the average of twice a year on all grades of pigments and in every instance the effective date of price change of each party has been the same. With respect to lithopone which is competitive with the calcium sulphate composite pigment, there has been maintained a constant differential. Unless the lithopone were priced below the titanium compound, it could not sell. Therefore, irrespective of costs of production the titanium compound has been priced 2 cents a pound above the price of lithopone. An honest technologist who knows that a better product can be made at a profit to undersell an inferior competing product cannot be expected to be happy in a situation which holds back the better and aids the poorer.

One of the worst features of cartel control lies in the overlapping of fields which is found in the case of large companies such as duPont and I. G. Farben. These companies are largely concerned not only with the production of pigments but also many other chemical products.

It is difficult to believe that the public interest has been adequately served by having the most valuable of white pigments subjected to complete control in this country and throughout the world by a cartel. What steps a free technology unfettered by cartel restrictions might have taken one cannot say with certainty. One may be quite sure that when the cartel shackles are broken, titanium will take its rightful place as not only the most important and useful of all pigments but also for a wide variety of other industrial uses.

10

Optical Instruments

How was it possible for Nazi Germany to emerge as a fully armed aggressor nation when she had been so thoroughly disarmed as a result of the Versailles Treaty? What can be done to prevent German technology from being utilized in preparation for another war? I propose in this chapter to discuss a particular cartel situation which sheds much light on the first question and will, I believe, be of value in finding an answer to the second.

There were, of course, many factors which contributed to the failure of the Versailles Treaty to accomplish the permanent peace which was contemplated at the time of its execution. It is my purpose to show herein that there was a definite program to sabotage the effectiveness of the Treaty and that that program was conceived in Germany almost as soon as the peace was made and many years before Hitler came into power. Furthermore, I shall prove, on the basis of documentary evidence, that evasion of the disarmament provisions of the Versailles Treaty was facilitated by a cartel agreement between a German firm and an American corporation. The agreement was between Carl Zeiss of Jena, Germany, and the Bausch and Lomb Optical Company of Rochester, New York.

In March, 1940, Bausch and Lomb and Carl Zeiss were indicted for violation of the antitrust laws. Pleas of *nolo contendere* were made, fines paid and thus trial of the indictment was avoided. A civil complaint and consent decree were filed in July 1940. The investigations in connection with this case revealed the following:

(1) Action was taken in 1921 to nullify the provisions of the Versailles Treaty which prohibited Germany from large scale manufacturing of military equipment.

(2) The parties caused Zeiss patents in this country to be taken out in the name of Bausch and Lomb, thus giving an appearance of American ownership and consequent protection against seizure by an Alien Property Custodian.

(3) Secret United States military information was given by Bausch and Lomb to Germans not only before but after Hitler came into power.

(4) Unknown to the Navy a secret commission to Bausch and Lomb was included in prices paid by the Navy for equipment furnished by Zeiss.

(5)Public declarations were made as to a policy of not selling military equipment to England and France for fear it might be used against this country, when the reason such policy existed was because of the provisions of a secret agreement with a German concern.

(6) Threats of patent infringement suits were used to frighten competing firms bidding upon military equipment for the United States Army.

(7) The cost to United States users of binoculars was greatly increased by reason of the efforts of Bausch and Lomb to protect itself from competition in that field.

No one factor is of greater importance in the waging of modern mechanized warfare than the precision instruments which indicate the exact location of a target and permit the accurate aiming of the gun or other device which will throw the projectile. The instruments which are in this category include periscopes, range finders, height finders, boresights, bombsights, telescopes, torpedo directors, gunsights, searchlight lenses and reflectors, as well as others. The glass which is used in making such instruments is of extremely high quality, it being absolutely essential that it be free from striae or streaks, bubbles, cloudiness and other defects which would impair its transparency or refractivity. At the outbreak of the first World War practically all such glass was made in Germany at the Schott glass works at Jena. Moreover, practically all first quality military optical instruments were also made in Germany, at Jena, in the factory of the Carl Zeiss Stiftung. The latter is a foundation created by bequests from Carl Zeiss and Dr. Ernest Abbe for the purpose of perpetuating the instrument business which their research had founded. By the time of the first World War it had grown into a tremendous establishment employing something like 10,000 people and supplying most of the Kaiser's war machine with optical-gunfire control instruments. Its continuance as a large scale producer of war instruments was entirely inconsistent with the aims and provisions of the Versailles Treaty.

Prior to the first World War Bausch and Lomb had been manufacturing military optical goods from glass imported from Germany. This had resulted from an agreement made in 1907. Carl Zeiss had threatened to establish a factory in the United States and sent a representative, Professor Tschopski, to this country in that connection. Apparently frightened by this threat, Bausch and Lomb entered into a series of transactions intended to eliminate any such competition. This was the so-called Optical Triple Alliance. The Fauth Instrument Company of which George Saegmuller was president was absorbed by Bausch and Lomb, and Saegmuller became vice-president of the latter firm. Carl Zeiss acquired one-fifth of Bausch and Lomb's capital stock and representation on its board of directors. Zeiss abandoned its plan to establish a factory in the United States, and Bausch and Lomb agreed to buy its glass for military optical instruments exclusively from Zeiss. In 1915 Zeiss refused to continue to supply Bausch and Lomb with glass, under their arrangements of 1907, because the Rochester firm had been supplying military instruments to countries which were at war with Germany. The Zeiss interest in Bausch and Lomb was purchased by members of the Bausch and Lomb families. Upon our entrance into the war in 1917 it was found that one of the most badly needed war materials was military optical goods. Neither the glass itself nor the instruments had been produced in this country in adequate quantities prior to the war. The Geophysical Laboratory, the Bureau of Standards, Bausch and Lomb, the Spencer Lens Co., and the Pittsburgh Plate Glass Co., worked strenuously on a program to produce adequate quantities of proper quality optical glass. Between April 1917 and November 1918 over 600,000 pounds of usable optical glass were produced, 65 per cent of it by Bausch and Lomb. Under the stress of war, the manufacture of military optical-gunfire control instruments was increased to the extent necessary to supply the fighting arms of the service.

Confronted with the restrictions imposed by the Versailles Treaty the heads of Carl Zeiss were more than glad to work out, in 1921, a secret agreement with Bausch and Lomb. To summarize this agreement, Zeiss placed its know-how at the disposal of Bausch and Lomb. The latter agreed to pay Zeiss a royalty starting at 7% and gradually diminishing for 25 years on all its military optical business except field glasses. As indicated quite plainly by the third paragraph of the agreement, the two companies divided up the world insofar as the sale of military optical goods was concerned:

"B. & L. obligate themselves not to sell, directly or indirectly, Military instruments to countries outside of the United States of America, and vice versa Carl Zeiss obligate themselves not to sell such instruments, directly or indirectly to the United States unless the parties have come to an agreement regarding the conditions of sale and the respective territories of distribution."

In the fourth paragraph, Zeiss was given the power to pass upon who should become the heads of the Bausch and Lomb "Military Department."

"In furtherance of the aims of this agreement B. & L. in Rochester will create a new Department solely responsible to the Board of Directors, which is charged with the independent development of all scientific and technical tasks within the Military scope and the maintenance of connections with Jena. The parties will come to an agreement as regards the heads to be placed in charge of this department."

In non-military fields the parties, while competing, were to give due regard to each other's interests. In the military field they agreed to full exchange of know-how and to rights under inventions acquired by them. The eighth paragraph anticipated the possibility of a conflict between the obligations to each other under the agreement and those owing to the nation: "The mutual obligation regarding the exchange of Military designs shall be void whenever the highest home Government of one party expressly demands that they be kept in confidence in the interest of the nation."

As will be shown, Zeiss subsequently demonstrated a very keen awareness of the privilege thus accorded it to obey Hitler's edicts and to keep its know-how in Germany. Bausch and Lomb on the other hand on more than one occasion weighed the demand for secrecy by our Army and Navy against the obligation to keep Zeiss informed and decided in favor of the latter. Both parties were fully aware of the fact that such an agreement had to be kept secret. It was intended to give Zeiss a new lease on life and actually made it possible for that concern to continue its existence in spite of the disarming of Germany and its war partners. The contract bluntly stated: "The contracting parties agree to keep the foregoing agreement in strict confidence as regards a third party and to guard silence concerning this agreement also with their own employees as far as this may be practical under the circumstances."

In contending that the contract was not secret, Bausch and Lomb states: "The original contract was shown to the U. S. Naval Observer in Berlin within a month of its execution, and through him the Bureau of Naval Intelligence and the Bureau of Ordnance were informed." As a matter of fact it seems clear that what was shown to our Naval representative in Berlin was not the "original contract" but only a portion of it with a certain other part withheld. The explanation for withholding part was that it related to matters which did not concern the Navy. The Navy representative was told that the Bausch and Lomb connection with Zeiss must be kept strictly confidential to protect Zeiss. The latter was not permitted under the terms of the Versailles Peace Treaty to continue the manufacture of military optical goods. In this connection a letter from George N. Saegmuller to Bausch and Lomb, sent from Jena on May 6, 1921, is of interest (Saegmuller was the vice-president of the firm who had gone to Germany to execute the agreement with Zeiss):

"I hope you rec'd our cable via Frankfurt in regard to the signing of the agreement Apr 29th and also my letter of even date in which I entered into the subject more fully. In that letter I stated that Capt. Bechler, Naval representative of the Am. Commission, telephoned for me to come to Berlin. This I intended to do but upon reflection I thought it best for him to come here as the various instruments in which they are interested are here. He assented to this and was to come yesterday but was taken sick so in place sent his aid, Lieut. Culbert, U. S. N., who was also accompanied by the Military represt. of the Am. Commission. What the Navy wants at once are: [enumerating range-finders, periscopes, sights and other similar instruments].

"For these instruments they are in a hurry and most probably we will have to import the optics from here as it would be impossible for us to produce them in time even with Zeiss opticians. I thought it best to go with Fred to Berlin to see Comdr. Bechler & impress upon him the importance of finding out how many of the various instruments are wanted, so as to receive the optics in time.

"*The Navy Department wants to obtain a copy of the agreement as a kind of a guarantee that if they order from us they will really receive Zeiss instruments or rather Zeiss quality. I told Lieut. Culbert that in my opinion there would be no difficulty in giving them a copy of the agreement which relates to military instruments. An entire copy we could not give as it relates to matters which does not concern the Navy; I wrote out what I thought and gave it to Dr. Fischer who will consult with the others; I don't think there will be any trouble on that score. I told both officers that our connection with Zeiss must be kept strictly confidential, chiefly on acc't of Zeiss; this they understand.*"

The reason it was necessary to keep the agreement secret is quite obvious but it need not be left to inference. On Dec. 27, 1930, Bausch and Lomb wrote to Interflash Signal Corporation of New York in reply to an inquiry concerning a range finder for the Grecian Navy Department. The letter contains this language:

"Our activities in the military line of instruments in general are concentrated in supplying the requirements of our own Government. While we have occasionally supplied foreign Governments with a few of these instruments, this has only been by chance as far as our facilities have permitted. We appreciate very much the offer of Admiral Dedes to become our special representative, but under the circumstances above stated we are unfortunately not in a position to accept this offer. We would suggest that he communicate with our friends, the Nederlandsche Instrumenten Compagnie, Den Haag, Holland, who manufacture the military line of optical instruments formerly made by Messrs. Carl Zeiss of Jena, Germany, *the latter not being permitted under the terms of the Peace Treaty to continue the manufacture of these products. . . .*"

On October 20, 1926, Bausch and Lomb wrote a letter to one of its representatives in the New York City office. J. A. Scheick of that office had quoted a price on two range finders to a New York firm which intended to ship them to Laredo, Texas for the ultimate use of the War Department of Mexico. The letter states:

"We have, on previous occasions, explained to Mr. Scheick that we must know the customer for whom this Military equipment is ultimately intended and we have also withdrawn our previous quotations stating that by reason of the limited supply of instruments on hand, it would be best to refer all such inquiries first to us, to find out whether or not we can take care of such an order. *The real reason, as you are aware, is our agreement with Zeiss, which, of course, we cannot explain to Mr. Scheick, as we are not only required to keep the nature of the agreement confidential, but the very existence of such an agreement.* As you are probably aware, this prevents us from making sales in the Military line, directly or indirectly, outside of the United States, unless by previous agreement with Zeiss on the price question; the price agreed to by Zeiss will be higher than their direct quotation. Obviously, we cannot accept the inclosed order intended for the War Department of Mexico."

The 1921 agreement was to run for 20 years with Bausch and Lomb obligated to continue to pay royalties for 25 years on all its military business whether based on Zeiss patents or not.

To carry out its agreement with Bausch and Lomb, Zeiss used the device of a corporation organized in Holland called N. V. Nederlandsche Instrumenten Compagnie—or Nedinsco, for short. It is a wholly owned subsidiary of Zeiss with its principal office at The Hague and its plant at Venlo, a town on the German border. Thus, in the years which passed before Hitler came into power, in the face of the disarmament provisions of the Versailles Treaty, Carl Zeiss was enabled to continue in the production of military optical equipment by merely moving its plant across the border. It was assured of and received royalties from all sales of such equipment in the United States by Bausch and Lomb, and assured of and received for Nedinsco freedom from competition in all the rest of the world so far as Bausch and Lomb was concerned. The survival of Carl Zeiss and its ability to provide at Jena one of the most important cogs in the Hitler war machine is clearly understandable and is in large part the result of the secret agreement of 1921.

The following paragraphs from a letter from Bausch and Lomb to Zeiss dated February 10, 1939, substantiates this statement:

"We are uncertain whether your reference to the more distant past is intended to cover the period between 1907 and 1915, during which time we freely admit that you were of assistance to us in the establishment of our military department, or to the period following the resumption of our cooperative endeavor after the World War.

"On the assumption that you are referring to the earlier period, we believe that you were completely compensated by the dividends which you received on the stock held in our company and by the appreciation in the value of this stock which you realized at the time of its sale.

"If, on the other hand, you are referring to the later period, *we believe that inasmuch as the arrangement made accomplished the primary objective of keeping your scientific staff intact at a time when you could not manufacture war materials, you were adequately compensated, particularly in view of the fact that, as you then knew, our Government was at that time very little interested in the development of, and made but very small appropriations for, fire control apparatus. In other words, we believe that the development work which you did during this period was primarily for your own benefit and not of great value to us here.*"

Here we see quite clearly how an American company aided a German company avoid both the spirit and the letter of the Versailles Treaty. Although Germany was prohibited from manufacturing and exporting military equipment, Bausch and Lomb "accomplished the primary objective of keeping your scientific staff intact at a time when you [Zeiss] could not manufacture war materials." In response to the letter just quoted, Zeiss replied on July 22, 1939:

"*In reference to 2.* In the reference to our letter of January 3, 1939, page 2, to a more remote time, that is, the time further back than 5 years, we have had reference to the first decade of the operation of the agreement as it now exists. Your assumption that during that time the development work done for you was above all to our advantage and had served the purpose of maintaining our design force is absolutely misjudged. *We had at no time the intention to allow our experience and knowledge of the military business to rest but have, as you know, established the Nedinsco branch for the express purpose so as to keep our place in the world market.* If the Nedinsco was a successful competitor where high grade equipment of our sphere of activities was in demand, this success is due to the work and efforts of our scientific staff and technicians who building on experiences before and during the war have explored all kinds of military spheres for our designs. The fruits of this successful, constructive labor has of course been reaped in general by Nedinsco. Surely we could not have continued the development work of even a small part of these activities from the small royalties received from you. From this follows definitely that you were the one who profited, without merit of your own, from the advantages of our complex and expensive development work, and that you unfortunately, notwithstanding repeated urging on our part, did not sufficiently make use of the given possibilities, a fact with which we found fault repeatedly verbally and in writing."

The sentence which I have italicized is a positive statement by Zeiss of its utter disregard of the conditions imposed by the Peace Treaty.

On June 27, 1925 a supplemental agreement was made which slightly changed the royalty provisions of the 1921 agreement. The division of world territory remained as before, except that the parties undertook to protect each other in bidding on government contracts by overbidding.

Subsequently on October 28, 1925, a further supplemental

agreement was signed by Zeiss at Jena and on December 11 by Bausch and Lomb at Rochester. After repeating the provisions of the supplemental agreement of June 27, 1925, it added:

"In case the inquiries referred to in paragraph 2 and 3 should not come to Bausch & Lomb from a Government, but exceptionally from a commercial house of a country outside of the United States, the firm of Bausch & Lomb is to communicate immediately with the firm of Nedinsco, and, depending on the situation at Nedinsco, either to make the protective offer named to her by the latter firm, or to decline the inquiry under pretense. The information in question will be given to the firm of Bausch & Lomb by the firm of Nedinsco."

The second supplemental agreement also contained the following provision:

"If the firm of Bausch & Lomb is furnishing to American shipyards, optical instruments as equipment for a ship of a country outside of the United States, all instruments in which the ideas of construction of the firm of Carl Zeiss have been used, shall, besides the trade name of Bausch & Lomb, be engraved with the designation, "System Nedinsco-Zeiss." Instruments according to the construction of Bausch & Lomb shall bear only their name. On instruments furnished by Nedinsco the name of Nedinsco will appear next to the name of Bausch & Lomb."

Thus, as early as 1925 there is evidence of the determination to place the Zeiss name back in the consciousness of the world. One more step was thereby taken to nullify the effect of the Versailles Treaty and to reestablish Germany in her place in the sun.

In 1926 Bausch and Lomb caused the 1921 agreement and its supplements to be modified because its counsel declared them to be wholly invalid as violating the antitrust laws. In place of the division of territory provision in the third paragraph, as quoted previously, the following language was inserted: "The license hereby granted is exclusive, the firm of Carl Zeiss agrees that it will grant no license to another American manufacturer."

This was a change in the language of the agreement to give an appearance of legality. Actually, after 1926, as well as before, the parties maintained a definite and illegal division of territory. The following sentences from a memorandum of Edward Bausch, dated January 27, 1927, show that no change in the actual relationship took place in the previous year: "It is my understanding, in accordance with the opinion of Carl Lomb, that we are not to bid on any military instruments for use anywhere outside of the U. S. The agreement is that if such inquiries come to us we are to refer them to Zeiss."

Paragraph 9 of the 1921 agreement, quoted above, providing for strict secrecy as to the agreement was dropped out as being (in 1926) unwise and unnecessary. In its place was inserted an innocuous provision that neither party has any claims against the other arising from previous agreements. This agreement of 1926, along with the early agreements which it purported to supersede was declared in violation of the antitrust laws by the decree entered by the court on July 9, 1940.

The 1921 agreement and also those which were subsequently executed contemplated an exchange of information and experience between the parties. This included the right of each party to send confidential representatives to the workshops of the other. Bausch and Lomb was more than anxious to have Zeiss employees visit its plant and its only complaint in connection with the visit of one such employee was that he had not been of great help to Bausch and Lomb while in this country. When Hitler came into power the American company found the door to the Zeiss designing rooms closed to it.

In a memorandum of April 19, 1938 Carl L. Bausch, Vice President of Bausch and Lomb, quoted paragraph VII of the contract providing for exchange of experience and access to the workshop and then stated: "In 1934, although they allowed me to go through their plant at Venlo, I could see none of the work that was being done at Jena, although all the design, part work and optical work was being done there at that time." In the same memorandum Mr. Bausch stated:

"My contention is that over the past five years we have paid out $139,000 without receiving any benefit from it except for the fact that our contract might have kept Zeiss out of this market. I doubt very much whether our government would have purchased any Zeiss range finders, even if Zeiss was allowed to solicit business."

In a letter from Carl Zeiss to Bausch and Lomb dated January 3, 1939 referring to the period of the past five years, i.e., since Hitler came into power, Zeiss said: "It certainly cannot be denied that we have been restricted in many respects in the execution of the agreement out of national interests particularly as far as visiting our plant is concerned."

In the matter of knowing what Zeiss was building for Hitler, of course, there was no passing of information to Bausch and Lomb. On the other hand, Zeiss was kept informed at least until well into the Hitler regime as to what was being ordered by our military departments. This was done not by sending the information directly to Zeiss but through Bausch and Lomb's German representative. August Lomb of Bausch and Lomb G.m.b.H. Frankfurt-on-the-Main acted as the conduit for the information. On July 9, 1929 Bausch and Lomb wrote to August Lomb as follows:

"We are appending our report which will bring the Military transactions up to date.

"We have nothing further to say at this time than what has already been stated in our report as regards the confidential nature of this information. Heretofore, the Government has merely been insistent that none of the details as regards the design of these instruments be made public, but lately it seems as if the quantities, prices, etc., and the amount of equipment purchased, etc., are also considered secret. *Obviously, our agreement with Messrs. Carl Zeiss cannot work satisfactorily unless, at least the latter information, becomes common knowledge to both parties, but some arrangement must be made whereby we are assured this information will be kept in strictest confidence.*"

The accompanying report is headed "Statement of Military Department to Mr. August Lomb, For the Months of April, May and June 1929." It gave the number of antiaircraft range finders, 26½ ft. range finders, periscopes, telescopes, and bombsights which it had delivered and discussed the items for which other bidders had been successful. Near the end of the report was this paragraph:

"It will be noted from the foregoing statements that not much information can be further obtained regarding competitive prices. While these bids are supposed to be public, it has lately become the practice to withhold the information from the public. Every letter and envelope from the Government is marked 'Confidential' and we are held accountable that the information will not become public, and that it will be treated in strictest confidence."

On December 20, 1932, Bausch and Lomb sent August Lomb a letter marked Military Department 8430 and enclosed a pamphlet dealing with submarine periscopes which he was to give to Zeiss and make sure that it was returned to him and by him to Bausch and Lomb. On the following day Bausch and Lomb wrote Zeiss this letter:

"We confirm having written you the letter stated in the above reference. The pamphlet referred to in it has been sent to Mr. August Lomb, via registered mail.

"It occurs to us that we were not sufficiently specific regarding the caution that must be exercised for our protection in keeping the loan of this pamphlet a secret, and particularly as regards the inspector. If any question should arise with regard to the pamphlet which you are preparing, *please do not admit to any one that this has been prepared analagous to our copy.*

"By reason of the great importance which we attach to the secrecy of this question, the copy has been sent via our Frankfurt office, and please make sure that after it has served its purpose it is again safely returned to our Mr. August Lomb."

The year 1933 — the year Hitler became Chancellor — brought a greatly enlivened interest on the part of Zeiss in the military secrets of our country. The following is a translation of a letter from Nedinsco to Bausch and Lomb dated April 7, 1933:

"Your last monthly report has given cause to the consideration that we surely would be better in a position to assist you *if you would report to us what kinds of instruments are under trial and in use by your military service.* There must be a great many questions regarding instruments for *airplanes, tanks, and ships* which demand special optical instruments.

"We would ask that you intensively *find out at the proper places and that you communicate to us the different problems,* so that we are placed in a position to name you the necessary instruments which we also make new to satisfy the actual dedemands.

"We believe that thereby the business could be enlivened and also work could be created for you as well as us."

A month later on May 11, 1933 Nedinsco again wrote to Bausch and Lomb as follows:

"We find, much to our regret, that the agreement during the course of the last few years has materialized exclusively in Rangefinders and Periscopes for the Navy and that also in this respect it has lost more and more in intensity, whereas all other instruments for Army and Navy have completely ceased.

"It may be assumed with great probability that the many other kinds of military instruments would find interest in the United States and that there would be a demand for these so that also for these there should be certain business chances.

"Notwithstanding that we transmitted to you information regarding many of our products, you have recently made a demand upon us for our constructive help only to a very limited extent.

"Business possibilities for foreign countries have never been mentioned which may result from American credits to foreign countries or from building contracts of American shipyards, gun factories, etc., and for which you might be considered as subcontractors. *Such business would according to Paragraph 3 of the agreement need a special understanding between us but is not excluded.* In view of the extremely serious economic situation in the world it would seem most urgent in our mutual interest that we endeavor to bring about a more intensive cooperation between us in the frame of our agreement and we therefore ask that you make known your position and make proposals as to how far and in what manner these relations could be furthered and the possibilities of business could be more rationally exploited.

"We would also be thankful for a comprehensive economic report which would enable us to judge conditions."

It can hardly be mere coincidence that these repeated requests for military information came so soon after Hitler's accession to power.

On December 14, 1933 Bausch and Lomb wrote to August Lomb as follows:

"We are sending you herewith our report which unfortunately had to be delayed by reason of the pressure of work which had to be taken care of in this department, due to the sudden activity brought about by the N. R. A.

"*By reason of special secrecy clauses of late attached to each bid and contract, these reports, as harmless as they are considering that they have a commercial purpose only, are contrary to these clauses. We cannot very well eliminate them under the existing agreement with Carl Zeiss; however the regulations are so stringent that particular care must be exercised to keep these reports in strictest confidence and they should be kept in a separate file under lock and key.*

"We would ask that you be governed accordingly and that you bring these facts to the attention of Messrs. Carl Zeiss."

August Lomb answered this letter on December 29, 1933. The first three paragraphs of his reply were as follows:

"Since writing you December 5th, your letter Nr. 8909 of December 14th was received. It just arrived before the writer went to Jena and could therefore be discussed there.

"*Monthly report.* That enclosed in your letter Nr. 8909 was therefore transmitted personally, impressing again the *necessity of considering this information strictly confidential and secret.* This is fully understood by the management as well as their Mil. Department and we *were again assured that these reports are locked up and only accessible to a few people who are fully responsible so that you can depend on your instructions being carried out.*

"The contents of this report were very pleasing so far as the important orders are concerned which you were able to secure. It is to be regretted that the thirty-four 11 ft. R.F. were lost, but evidently other firms also have to expect part of the business."

It would no doubt have been very reassuring to our War and Navy Departments to know that these reports were "only accessible to a few people" in Hitler's Germany.

On October 16, 1934 Bausch and Lomb wrote to August Lomb as follows:

"We are very sorry to find that we neglected to send you our report for a considerable length of time. *As you know, we are not free to give you these reports.* This is about the best excuse that we can offer; *the less reports we make the less the chance of any going astray.*

"We shall try to keep you informed more regularly having your assurance that these matters will be treated by you and Carl Zeiss in strictest confidence."

The report of October 16, 1934 entitled "Statement of Military Department to Mr. August H. Lomb" lists the number and kinds of range finders delivered each month and also the total number of various types of instruments, orders for which Bausch and Lomb has booked since their last report. There is also the remark that they lost an order for four 13½ ft. height finders awarded to Keuffel and Esser (another American firm). This report contains the following remarkable statement in connection with designs for submarine periscopes:

"Our design force now consists of thirteen men all occupied on present contracts so that it cannot be assumed that we want to throw the burden of the design work on Carl Zeiss. *As a matter of fact we could not do this under the secrecy clauses of the 'Recovery Act,' but surely we ought to be able to rely on Carl Zeiss for support when and where it is most important.*

We are hopeful that the promise made in letter of October 5 to give us this design by next spring can be considerably improved, in fact that every effort will be made to bring the solution of this problem to a point which will enable us to enter into competition in the next bid."

On October 20, 1936 Bausch and Lomb wrote the following letter to Carl Zeiss:

"With your letter in reference we received from you a new optical layout in the form of your drawing A 33 08 65/Opt. L. No. 2 for the altiperiscopes of 34 foot optical length.

"We recently learned that our Government is now contemplating the use of 40 foot submarine periscopes and that bids for these will soon be submitted for consideration. These periscopes will be built according to the identical specifications as those you have in your possession with the exception that, as already stated, the optical length has been increased from 34 feet to 40 feet and the reduced section has been increased in length as shown on our drawing Mil. 458 sent herewith. Moreover, the inner diameter of the main body tube now measures 6,500 inches diameter for a distance of 11 feet from the eyepiece and while its remaining length has an inner diameter of 6.375 inches as shown on our drawing Mil. 458.

"We would ask that you kindly prepare for us immediately a new optical layout conforming to these changes and that you give us this information at the earliest possible date. As stated this question will soon need our consideration and unless we have the data available by that time we shall have to forego bidding on this new proposition."

August Lomb realized the situation in which Bausch and Lomb was placed in sending written reports of secret military information to Germany. In a letter of July 9, 1937 to Bausch and Lomb he made this very helpful suggestion:

"Prior to the years 1935 and 1936 Zeiss have always received a list of numbers, kinds and prices of the instruments furnished during one year when the commission statement for the respective year was rendered. *Since 1935 such a statement was not received, probably because you did not want to furnish any such data in accordance with your letter Nr. 9383 of October 16th, 1934. Zeiss, however, would be satisfied with very brief and condensed information, for instance Range Finders abbreviated to R.F. etc., if possible.*

"Of course you will have to consider this with the Executive Office and may let us know occasionally whether feasible or not."

In a letter of March 24, 1939—the week after Hitler invaded Czechoslovakia—Carl Zeiss made this demand upon Bausch and Lomb:

"For this purpose it is *absolutely necessary*, and that is why we ask you for it, *that you supply us*, before we arrive at our final decision, with a *precise statement of those patents of ours which you use in your manufacturing processes, designating at the same time those instruments in whose manufacture these patents are used, also indicating the turnover you have had in these instruments during the last two business years, and the volume of orders which you have at present on hand for such instruments.*

"We take it for granted that your Administrative Division can make up such a statement without trouble and loss of time so that we *may expect it within a month at the latest.*"

Instead of the detailed reports which had formerly been sent, Bausch and Lomb complied with this demand by giving a statement of the aggregate amount of sales of instruments covered by Zeiss patents in 1937 and in 1938, designating the patents. They stated they had orders for future delivery of instruments covered by Zeiss patents totaling approximately $1,000,000 and giving the patent numbers.

From the foregoing quotations it seems rather clear that Bausch and Lomb put their own interpretation—and a strange one—upon their obligation to keep military information secret and confidential.

The supplemental agreement of June 27, 1925 contained the following provision:

"In the case of inquiries, received by Bausch & Lomb from authorities outside of the United States of America, by Carl Zeiss from the authorities of the United States, one party informs the other of the inquiry and is *obligated to make the protective offer named by the other party. The increase of the protective offer over the normal price for the corresponding quantity of instruments in question shall not be higher than 20%*. Both parties are obligated to treat such inquiries as promptly as possible. *If the party, that has made the protective offer should, nevertheless, receive the order, it is obligated to cede in full to the other firm the excess price representing the protection.* The firm of Bausch & Lomb besides, has to pay to the firm of Zeiss the royalty on the normal price according to paragraph 2, in case Bausch & Lomb is awarded the order."

This arrangement served the purpose of making a governmental authority—United States or some other—believe that bona fide bids were being made in response to requests. Such collusive bidding is a fraud upon the government and while a similar provision was included in the supplemental agreement of October 28, 1925, it was omitted from the agreement of 1926. And yet in 1932 there is evidence of willingness on the part of Bausch and Lomb to be less than forthright in dealing with the Navy Department. The following excerpt is from a letter from Bausch and Lomb to Carl Zeiss dated February 24, 1932:

"From the copy of the above contract which we have sent you with our other letter of today, Mil. Dept. 8077, you will take notice that the contract provides that customs entry will be taken care of by the Government. *In view of this, and in order not to divulge to the Navy Department that we earn a commission of 10% on this transaction, it will be necessary that the consular invoices and export declarations which you will have to make out be higher in this particular case than your net invoice prices to us. Your shipping papers, consular invoices, and export declarations, etc., accordingly should state the following prices*, f.o.b. Venlo:

Item	*Unit*	*Total*
1 —The unit price to be declared by you will be	$7,400	$14,800.00
1a—The unit price to be declared by you will be	470	470.00
2 —The unit price to be declared by you will be (Note: The repeater motor is here included)	6,780	20,340.00
2a—The unit price to be declared by you will be	470	940.00

"The difference between the above prices and those stipulated in the official contract are satisfactorily explained by shipping expenses, etc.

"It goes without saying that you will bill us for these periscopes in accordance with your letter of December 29, 1931 (N XIII/6661), less 10% commission."

The provisions of the 1921 and 1925 agreements prevented

Bausch and Lomb from selling to any purchaser outside the United States unless such sale was approved by Zeiss. That the omission of this provision from the agreement of 1926 did not mean a change in policy is clearly shown by the following memoranda exchanged by two Bausch and Lomb officials:

"From: Mr. M. H. Eisenhart Date: Jan. 11, 1927.

"To: Mr. Edw. Bausch.

"I have read the following paragraph in August Lomb's letter of December 20, 1926:

" 'We note that you have decided to give up all military work in connection with foreign countries, thus doing away with the supplementary agreement of October 28th, 1925. Its second paragraph on page 2 treats of instruments which you might be called to supply for foreign vessels built or equipped on American ship yards, as was the case for Argentine. We understand that, as this entire agreement is now canceled, you will renounce to bidding for such instruments hereafter.'

"Is it your understanding from this that in the future we will not bid on any military instruments for use anywhere outside of the United States? As this is a change over our present procedure, I think we want to be sure of the definite understanding."

* * *

"From: Mr. E. Bausch Reply Date: Jan. 27, 1927.

"To: Mr. M. H. Eisenhart

"It is my understanding, in accordance with the opinion of Carl Lomb, that we are not to bid on any military instruments for use anywhere outside of the U. S. The agreement is that if such inquiries come to us we are to refer them to Zeiss. If, on the other hand, any inquiries come to them which belong to this territory, they are to be referred by them to us. A condition may arise, as has been the case before, where a foreign government might want to place an order with us, this to be under supervision of Army and Navy officers and the inspection as well. The procedure then would be—I should think—that we defer giving any definite answer until we had submitted the matter, according to agreement, to Zeiss, and await their disposition of it."

The Edward Bausch who wrote the latter memorandum is the same gentleman who was quoted in the *Literary Digest* of December 12, 1936 in the following item:

"Millions of dollars of foreign Government orders for military optical instruments have been rejected by the Bausch & Lomb Co., of Rochester, New York, because they might conceivably be used against the United States or its interests in another War.

"Proudly last week, vigorous, eighty-two-year-old Dr. Edward Bausch, founder and chairman, declared that to be his company's settled policy, developed 'through a close understanding with the Departments of the Army and the Navy of our Government.' . . .

"Chiefly, Bausch & Lomb's rejected orders have been offered by England and France, have been for range-finders, periscopes, gun-sights, binoculars, artillery fire-control instruments. Business from those two Governments would have exceeded $1,500,000. Various smaller nations have also sought to make contracts and have been refused. Self-sufficient Germany, however, has shown no needs.

"*War-Time Seller*—During the World War, encouraged by Washington, Bausch & Lomb made large sales to the Allies, built up an extensive business with Great Britain. Promptly with the reappearance of European war-scares several years ago, however, the policy of no supplies to potential combatants abroad was adopted. 'They are not prepared for war over there,' a company officer gravely explained last week, 'and if we refuse to help them prepare, it puts it off just that much.'"

In the documents taken from Bausch and Lomb's files there are dozens of letters in which inquiries from foreign buyers of military optical instruments were answered by Bausch and Lomb with an expression of disinterest and a reference to Nedinsco. On March 30, 1938 Bausch and Lomb wrote the British Military Attache in Washington as follows:

"In reply to your letter of March 24, 1938 we wish to inform you that the instruments that we manufacture for the U. S. War Department are 4 meter Stereo Height Finders.

"Unfortunately we have to inform you that we are not in a position to take British Government orders at the present time."

On June 20, 1938 the International Standard Electric Corporation of New York wrote Bausch and Lomb with regard to procuring manufacturing equipment for its English associate, Standard Telephone and Cables, Ltd., to manufacture certain lenses and optical systems from British optical glass. After some conferences and consideration, Bausch and Lomb wrote to International Standard Electric Corporation on July 1, 1938 as follows:

"One of the first steps I took in giving consideration to your proposition which we discussed yesterday was to look into the contractual arrangements to which we are already obligated which I spoke to you about in my conversation.

"*Our attorneys tell us that we are absolutely tied up in a way that will prevent our giving you the type of assistance you need to get into the manufacture of optical fire control instruments.* My thought was that events over the last few years had changed our foreign relationship in a way that might allow us to work with you, but I am definitely satisfied now that such is not the case. Because of this situation, there is no need for us to delay you any further in your plan.

"I enjoyed very much your visit here and perhaps at some future occasion I may have the opportunity of meeting you again."

In the October 1940 number of *Fortune Magazine* which contained an article about Bausch and Lomb there was a two-page spread devoted to "The Critical Geography of Industries Essential to U. S. Rearmament." With reference to optical goods, this statement appeared: "After aircraft engines, armor plate, and machine tools this little industry (range finders, aircraft height finders) stands fourth among defense bottlenecks."

There are undoubtedly many factors which contributed to defense bottlenecks. It seems quite certain that the Zeiss-Bausch and Lomb restrictive arrangement has had a substantial part in bringing about this condition. There is no way of ascertaining how many times competitors were intimidated by threats from the combination of the two companies which were the largest in the world. The following quotation is taken from a letter from Bausch and Lomb to Carl Zeiss dated June 12, 1932 and referring to a new order for Height Finders for which the Frankford Arsenal was contemplating asking bids:

"Bids for this new prospective order have not yet been received by us. It is at present our intention after the bids have been received to *wait until a few days before the opening of the bids* and then call the attention of the Keuffel & Esser Company to the fact that we are controlling patent No. 1638190 which prohibits their furnishing the Height Finder in question. *In this manner we hope to be able to make them afraid of touching this business.* You will understand, therefore, how anxious we are to receive your opinion that the arrangement of four compensator wedges on one side of the Range [sic] Finder infringes your patent."

The foregoing quotation indicates one of the reasons for the arrangement by which all Zeiss inventions were to be patented in the United States by Bausch and Lomb. There can be little doubt that American patentees of competing military optical instruments would have much more to fear in infringement litigation initiated by the American firm of Bausch and Lomb than would be the case if the real owner of the patents, the German firm of Carl Zeiss, were the patentee. The other reason for this arrangement was the fear that Zeiss-owned patents would again be confiscated by the United States Government as had been done in the first World War. For the two reasons and possibly others it was clearly understood that all Zeiss inventions patented in the United States should result in patents issuing to Bausch and Lomb. What was just as clearly understood was that at the expiration of their contract all these patents were to be reassigned to Zeiss. This was stated in many documents one of which, a letter from Bausch and Lomb to Zeiss, dated January 17, 1936, should suffice to substantiate the point.

"We have given consideration to the suggestions which you have made for further clarification of the interpretations of the existing contract which was the subject of our letter of October 14, 1935. We are, therefore, restating the points covered in that letter, as follows:

[Par. 1 and 2 deals with termination of the contract]

"3. You are to assign to us all unexpired United States patents and all pending applications for United States patents in the military field now standing in your name or the name of any company controlled by you through stock ownership or otherwise, or in the name of any individual in the employ of your company or any company so controlled by you. You are also to assign to us all applications for patents in the military field which are filed prior to October 31, 1940, on inventions made by any individual or individuals employed by you or any company so controlled by you. You are to file and prosecute such applications and pay all expenses and fees therefor. With respect to such pending and future applications we suggest that you execute the proper assignment and send it to us as soon as you receive the notice of allowance in an application. We will promptly record the assignment in the United States Patent Office and notify you so that you may pay the final fee in due time so as to have the patent issued in our name as assignee. *We shall assign to you or your nominee all your United States patents or pending applications which have been taken out in our name, or caused to be assigned to us under the provisions of said agreement prior to April 30, 1941, reserving to ourselves only the license to manufacture thereunder upon the payment to you of the royalty as agreed under 2 hereinabove.*"

Field glasses or binoculars were expressly excepted from the cartel arrangement between Zeiss and Bausch and Lomb. In 1931 Bausch and Lomb bid $39.50 each on a United States Navy request for bids on 600 binoculars. Zeiss bid $26, and this angered Bausch and Lomb to the extent that they brought about a greatly increased tariff rate on imported binoculars. The correspondence between the two firms over a period of years refers to this episode. Edward Bausch of Bausch and Lomb wrote to August H. Lomb in Frankfurt on November 18, 1932. The last two paragraphs of his letter are as follows:

"In all other departments we find the Zeiss competition keen and aggressive. Zeiss have established themselves in this country and have been for years making more and more intensive efforts to get business. As an instance of their efforts we will cite the circumstance of their having put in a bid for Field Glasses to the government at such ridiculously low prices that we cannot understand how there can be any profit in it for them, but leaves us with a feeling that they are aiming to put us out of competition and acquire the business for themselves.

"Such efforts as they are making in this territory will surely lead to more aggressive action on our part and will certainly lead to anything but friendly feeling, and ultimately, to a more serious situation."

On February 6, 1934, Zeiss wrote Edward Bausch as follows:

"I received your letter of January 25, and at the same time, a report from our Dr. Bauer about his interview with you and your associates on January 15, 1934 in Rochester. First of all, I wish to thank you for having gone to the trouble to write down the sequence of events, which brought about the change in duty calculation on our prism binoculars, with the result that the duty, which will actually have to be paid, comes very close to doubling the present rate. I expressed myself to Mr. Lomb in a very general way, and had pointed out merely the effect of the change of duty, which was probably caused by your initiative, and I used the expression that the sixty per cent rate had, in reality, been doubled.

"The essential consequence is that quality binoculars—and only those of more than 5x magnification, and of foreign net value of more than $12—have been affected by this measure. In reality, only Zeiss Binoculars fall under this arrangement, whereas all the cheap French prism binoculars, which are not negligible in quantity, are exempt.

"From your letter, I have noted that the steps taken by you were prompted by our offer and that of Carl Zeiss, New York, of six hundred 6 x 30 prism binoculars at $26 each, which we made in 1931 to the Navy. I believe that I do not have to add anything to the explanations which our Dr. Bauer has given you concerning this matter. The thought occurs to me, however, whether it would not have been appropriate, in view of the friendly and long relations between our respective houses, if one of your gentlemen had communicated with our Dr. Bauer and had pointed out the low prices to him in order to bring about a satisfactory solution of the question for the future, and this by means of a friendly understanding. Such an understanding would have been readily possible at the time, for we have always been ready to recognize justified wishes or requests of other houses, especially of those friendly to us.

"I would consider it to our mutual interests if this duty arrangement, which, as I admit frankly, has caused great bitterness on our part, would disappear again. As you know from several negotiations on other matters here and there, we and Dr. Bauer are always ready for a price agreement, which protects your just interests."

On February 28, 1935, Bausch and Lomb wrote to Dr. Bauer of Carl Zeiss, Inc., New York. The first paragraph of his letter is as follows:

"Although I enjoyed my visit with you last Saturday morning very much, I have not been able to get out of my mind your statement that you have not confidence in the younger generation here in Rochester. Since this is predicated, I believe, entirely upon the binocular situation, I just want to repeat again what I told you in New York, that I believe whatever action we took in regard to the tariff on binoculars was prompted entirely by the fact that you bid a figure on a Navy contract for binoculars which was absolutely out of reason and made it look to us as if you were going to get this binocular business from the United States Navy at any price. When we saw there was no possibility of getting business from our own

Navy at a reasonable figure, we took the only step that was open to us and made a complaint to one of our senators that started a Senate Investigation and finally culminated in an executive order that resulted in changing the method of figuring tariff to the basis of American valuation."

On March 8, 1935, K. A. Bauer of Carl Zeiss, Inc., wrote Bausch and Lomb. The first three paragraphs of his letter are as follows:

"I thank you for your letter of February 28, referring to our conversation of February 23rd. I wish to correct your impression of my having made the general statement 'that I have no confidence in the younger generation in Rochester.' I said: 'How can we have confidence, that an agreement regarding Contact glasses—if possible at all—will turn out satisfactorily, after the experience we had in the binocular matter?' I also said that under the management of the older generation, such a thing, as this binocular case turned out to be, would not have been possible. But I do not wish these words to be generalized to the above blunt statement, and I am sorry, if I may not have expressed myself clearly enough.

"Now turning to the binocular matter, you know that I have had conversations with your firm in which I found a certain degree of understanding for the untenability of the present tariff situation and a willingness not to resist a reasonable solution. Due to the political constellation and to tariff negotiations pending in Washington with other countries, the flexible tariff clause is at present petrified and nobody can say, when this may change. In the meantime, importation of highgrade binoculars continues to be impossible. As long as this condition lasts, we shall naturally feel irritated and we cannot but resent the fact that it was brought about by methods which we must condemn. The nature of the tariff action was camouflaged by the wording of the Senate Resolution, in order to deceive the importers of prism binoculars. We ourselves as well as other importers were deprived of what little right we had under the tariff law to state our side. If you personally have any doubt as to who engineered this whole affair, I suggest that you read the stenographic report of the so-called 'Public Hearing' which took place in Washington on October 18, 1932.

"You say that we quoted on 600 binoculars 6 x 30 such a low price that it was 'out of reason.' Admitted that our price of $26—was low. Your quotation of $39.50, however, seems to be exorbitant. It is also true that the quality specified by the Navy was of a higher grade than that of commercial binoculars. But this fact is more than compensated by the large number of 600 glasses involved, which were to be manufactured, shipped and delivered at one time to one party, whose credit is beyond doubt. The large number called for a special low price. Instead you quoted to the U. S. Navy—your best single customer—considerably more than what you asked from a dealer for one single glass. At that time you sold your 6 x 30 model (with central focusing device) at $66 list, and at $35.18 and even at $33 net to the trade; a few months later at even lower prices. If you deduct from these prices an adequate amount for the central focusing device, which the Navy did not require, your net trade price for one single 6 x 30 binocular with individual focusing would have come rather close to our price of $26. What difference remained might have been cut down further by the quantity factor as explained above. Had your firm quoted as one should have expected, considering all that has been said above, we would have had no chance whatever to get the order under the Budget Law even at a lower price. In our opinion you bid too high, expecting that under the Budget Law you would have the monopoly anyhow."

One recalls the urgent plea which was made about the time of Pearl Harbor for all private citizens to make gifts of their binoculars for use by the armed service. To the extent that a shortage of such material can be traced to the squabbles among cartelists it is a condition which should certainly never be allowed to recur.

One of the most serious problems which will confront our government and the United Nations in connection with the termination of the war with Germany is that of eliminating for the future the German war machine. The relations of Carl Zeiss and Bausch and Lomb show what may be expected when private business concerns are permitted to handle such a problem as though it were a matter of private concern. Surely it is to be hoped that the policy of our government as expressed in the peace which will be made with Germany will not be rendered ineffectual because of the private international policy of certain business concerns. The decree of July 9, 1940, enjoined Bausch and Lomb from further carrying out any of the provisions of its agreements with Carl Zeiss. This alone is not sufficient to insure that the public policy expressed by government action shall not be thwarted by the machinations of private cartels.

11

Miscellaneous Products

Three recent cases illustrate some interesting characteristics of the cartel problem. These cases—involving cartelization of pharmaceutical products, chemicals, firearms and ammunition, and matches—include industrial concerns and individuals in Germany, England, Canada, Sweden, Chile, the Argentine, and Brazil. They are significant not only because of their inherent character, but also because the war has not materially affected their operation. True, the war forced certain changes upon them, but these were modifications, not cessations.

Since the cases in question had not been legally adjudicated at the time this was written, it is well for the reader to remember that the statements which follow are allegations which were a matter for litigation between the government and the various defendants.

On October 28, 1943, the Department of Justice filed a complaint charging Merck & Co., Inc., of Rahway, N. J., the largest producer of pharmaceutical chemicals in the United States, and E. Merck Chemical Works, of Darmstadt, Germany, with maintaining a cartel agreement in violation of the antitrust laws.

Named as defendants in the suit were Merck & Co.; George W. Merck, President of the firm; and Powers-Weightman-Rosengarten Corp., a Merck subsidiary. The complaint charged that:

(1) The Rahway firm and its subsidiary conspired with the Darmstadt concern to divide world territory into non-competitive areas by means of what they themselves describe as a "Treaty," dated November, 1932.

(2) Under the terms of this "Treaty," the Rahway firm was assigned the United States and Canada as exclusive territory, while the Darmstadt organization was assigned almost all the rest of the world. The "Treaty" also provided that Cuba, the West Indies and the Philippines were joint territory in which conditions of sale and prices were fixed by agreement.

(3) Since the British blockade after outbreak of the war in 1939 prevented the Darmstadt firm from exporting to many foreign countries, particularly to Latin America, it was agreed that the American company would supply Darmstadt's agents in South America but that the territorial provisions of the 1932 "Treaty" remained in effect, with Latin American markets to be returned to Merck of Darmstadt as exclusive territory after the war.

(4) To carry out this agreement Merck of Rahway revived a dormant subsidiary, Powers-Weightman-Rosengarten Corporation, to engage during the war in export business in territory assigned exclusively to Merck-Darmstadt. The purpose of using this dormant subsidiary was to enable Merck of Rahway more easily to abandon its export business in Darmstadt's territory after the war.

(5) Merck of Rahway not only intends to abandon all its export business in Darmstadt's territory after the war but to

continue the territorial division provided in the 1932 "Treaty" until 1982.

(6) The agreement covers approximately 400 pharmaceuticals and chemicals, including quinines, sulfa drugs, vitamins, narcotics and mercurials.

The government charges specifically that prior to the last war there were close ties between Merck of Rahway and Merck-Darmstadt which were dissolved in 1919 by the Alien Property Custodian. During the last war the American Merck company gained a large export business in chemicals and pharmaceuticals in Central and South America only to relinquish this business and allow it to be recaptured by Merck-Darmstadt after the war.

In 1932, the two companies entered into understandings and agreements to divide world markets into exclusive areas, and as a device to conceal these arrangements they entered into a so-called "Treaty Agreement" on November 17, 1932, for a period of 50 years. The German and American Merck companies, it is charged, divided the use of the "Merck" trade name and the sales of their products throughout the world. Under this arrangement, the right to sell exclusively in the United States and Canada was assigned to Merck of Rahway, which was also permitted to sell jointly with Merck-Darmstadt in Cuba, the West Indies and the Philippines. The rest of the world became the exclusive sales territory of the German company.

In making the above charges, the Government asked the Court to dissolve the 1932 "Treaty Agreement"; to cancel the exclusivity of licenses to use certain patents of the German firm; to enjoin Merck of Rahway from refusing to fill orders from established chemical and pharmaceutical dealers in foreign countries; and to enjoin the American firm from vesting any patent rights in the German company at any future time without first notifying the Attorney General of its intention to make such patent transfer; and to prevent the parties from entering any similar agreements or arrangements.

* * *

On January 6, 1944, the Department of Justice filed a complaint charging two American companies, a British company, the American agent of the British company, and five of their officers, with maintaining an international cartel agreement to restrain trade in the manufacture of chemical products, firearms, and ammunition, in violation of the Sherman Antitrust Act.

Named as defendants in the suit were: E. I. du Pont de Nemours and Company, Inc., Wilmington, Delaware, including Lammot du Pont, Chairman of the Board, Walter Samuel Carpenter, Jr., President; Remington Arms Company, Inc., Bridgeport, Connecticut, including Charles Krum Davis, President and General Manager; Imperial Chemical Industries, Ltd., London, England, including Harry Duncan McGowan, Chairman of the Board, and Henry Mond, Deputy Chairman; and Imperial Chemical Industries (New York), Ltd., New York City, American agent of ICI.

The government charged that beginning sometime prior to 1920 du Pont, ICI and, from 1933, Remington, had been engaged in a conspiracy and combination in restraint of trade and commerce in chemical products, arms, including war materials, and ammunition in the United States and with foreign nations, and were parties to contracts and agreements in violation of the Sherman Antitrust Act.

The alleged conspiracy consisted of an agreement, the terms of which were:

(1) That du Pont and ICI not compete with each other.

(2) That du Pont, Remington and ICI cooperate to eliminate competition between Remington and ICI.

(3) That du Pont and ICI each be assigned certain marketing areas as exclusive territory.

(4) That the defendants agree to eliminate competition between themselves in non-exclusive territory by various arrangements, including the formation of joint companies, to sell their products in accordance with agreed quotas and prices.

(5) That du Pont and ICI exchange exclusive licenses under all patents and processes for the exclusive territories allocated to each, and non-exclusive licenses for the remainder of the world.

(6) That du Pont and ICI attempt to obtain for each other the benefit of agreements and understanding arrived at with third parties for allocation of world markets or the acquisition of technological developments.

(7) That du Pont and ICI cooperate to eliminate the competition of other companies throughout the world.

The agreement was estimated to affect thousands of products, ranging from explosives to paints and varnishes. Du Pont is the largest manufacturer of chemical products in the United States, with total assets approximating one billion dollars, including the ownership of approximately 23 per cent of the stock of General Motors Corporation. Remington is described as the largest manufacturer of sporting arms and ammunition in the United States, and since 1933 has been controlled by du Pont.

Imperial Chemical Industries, which has a virtual monopoly of the chemical industry in Great Britain, was formed as the result of a merger of four major British companies, and it was contended that ICI's founders intended not only to gain a monopoly of the chemical industry in the United Kingdom but to join with the other major manufacturers of chemicals throughout the world, including I. G. Farbenindustrie of Germany and du Pont, to safeguard such monopoly position. This policy was explained by ICI to du Pont as follows:

"Sir Harry explained that the formation of I.C.I. is only the first step in a comprehensive scheme which he has in mind to rationalize chemical manufacture in the world. The details of such a scheme are not worked out, not even in Sir Harry's own mind, but the broad picture includes working arrangements between three groups—the I. G. in Germany, Imperial Chemical Industries in the British Empire, and du Pont and the Allied Chemical & Dye in America. The next step in the scheme is an arrangement of some sort between the Germans and the British."

Imperial Chemical Industries (New York) conducts no independent business operations of its own but acts solely as agent for ICI for the transaction of business in the United States. The complaint stated that in 1935 the then president of ICI (New York) described the corporation as the "private commercial legation" of ICI.

Sometime prior to 1920 du Pont and ICI came to an understanding with each other for the elimination of competition in the sale of explosives in all parts of the world. By this understanding du Pont was allocated the United States and Central America as its exclusive sales territory, and ICI was allocated the balance of the world, with the exception of Canada, Newfoundland and South America. Both companies were to refrain from manufacture in or export to each other's exclusive markets, while Canada, Newfoundland and South America were to be shared by both companies on a non-competitive basis.

It was further agreed that profits from the sale of commercial explosives in South America would be divided equally; and that in Canada the firm of Canadian Industries, Ltd., jointly owned by both, would be utilized to eliminate competition between them. Moreover, it was agreed that du Pont and ICI would exchange exclusive licenses under all their present and future patents, processes and inventions for use in the exclusive territory of each, and that non-exclusive licenses would be exchanged for the territories shared by both companies.

By 1925, however, Dynamit Aktiengesellschaft (known as DAG), a German corporation, had begun to offer serious competition to du Pont and ICI in all important world markets, and in that year the two companies reached an agreement with DAG to eliminate competition in commercial explosives. By this understanding, DAG agreed to abstain from doing business in certain markets and to adhere to quota arrangements in other markets including South America. For this agreement, DAG was awarded as its exclusive market in commercial explosives Germany, Holland, Poland, Austria, Denmark and Bulgaria. Du Pont and ICI also subsequently acquired a stock interest in DAG.

In order to carry out the understanding, it was charged, du Pont, ICI and DAG about 1925, organized Explosives Industries, Ltd., incorporated under the laws of the United Kingdom. Du Pont and ICI were each allocated 37½ per cent of its shares, and DAG 25 per cent; and the parties agreed to conduct all their exports in explosives to South America through this corporation. Exports to Chile and Bolivia were not included, however, as du Pont and ICI had earlier organized a jointly-owned company, Compania Sud-Americana de Explosives, to import and manufacture explosives in Bolivia and Chile.

At the time du Pont and ICI entered into the conspiracy, it was asserted, they were primarily explosives manufacturers, but both continually increased the number of products manufactured until explosives became but one of many items. The growth of the combination paralleled the growth of the companies; as each company made new products, they were brought into the conspiracy.

The complaint cited as an example of the functioning of the conspiracy that during the period 1920-29, du Pont tried to protect ICI from the competition of American cartridge companies by withdrawing from these companies discounts and rebates in connection with the sale of powder so that they might not disrupt ICI's markets by cutting prices.

By 1929 the conspiracy had incorporated substantially all of the products then made by du Pont and ICI, and the complaint alleged that in 1929 a further agreement was entered into whereby all products other than explosives would be handled in the British Empire by ICI and in the United States and Central America by du Pont. It was further agreed that as to the balance of the world, the two companies would enter into special arrangements to eliminate competition and would explore the desirability of utilizing joint companies. Later, two joint companies were founded to handle products in Argentina and Brazil —Industrias Quimicas Argentinas "Duperial," S. A., and Industrias Chimicas Brazeileiras "Duperial," S. A.

Military explosives had been omitted from the 1929 agreement, as the two companies continued to make certain special arrangements to eliminate competition between them. After 1933, when Remington joined the conspiracy, the complaint states that further contracts and agreements were entered into to eliminate competition between ICI and Remington in the manufacture and sale of ammunition and sporting arms.

The parties clearly understood that they would continue the relationship between them irrespective of governmental action which might affect the concerns. In July, 1933, Lord McGowan wrote to Lammot du Pont as follows:

"I have warned my people that no fiscal alterations in the

U. S. A. must be allowed to affect the interpretation to be placed on our Patents and Processes Agreement, and the working out of the co-operation for which the Agreement provides. . . . I find it is a good thing to issue such warnings . . . so that everything possible is done to ensure that no prospective political or legislative action on the part of Governments is permitted to influence relations between du Pont and ICI."

To this letter, Mr. du Pont replied in part: "I feel the same; . . . If any legislation or international agreements are brought about which affect these ICI-du Pont relations, I am sure we will be able to adjust ourselves so as to get the continued benefit of our Agreement."

The agreement of 1929 was to expire in June, 1939, and at that time ICI and du Pont entered into another agreement for 10 years and indefinitely thereafter. The territorial provisions were continued, and in addition to the patents and products covered by the 1929 agreement, numerous other products were added, including cellulose compounds, alkali metals and their products, fertilizers, dyestuffs, synthetic resins and plastics, perfumes, flavoring compounds, pharmaceutical chemicals, and new synthetic products, including rubber, nylon and neoprene.

The Government charged that competition was restrained successfully by means of the joint companies in Canada, Argentina and Brazil, pointing out that because I. G. Farben was encroaching on the field in Argentina, certain arrangements were made for a further joint company to be partly controlled by Farben. However, because of the war this procedure was not carried out, although du Pont's Foreign Relations Department stated in February, 1940, that "the du Pont Company informed I. G. that they intended to use their good offices after the war to have the I. G. participation restored."

The purpose of the Government's suit was to bring about the

abrogation of the illegal contracts, to secure a perpetual injunction against ICI from violating the American Antitrust Acts, and to require du Pont and ICI to take further steps to prevent future use of joint companies.

* * *

On May 1, 1944, the Department of Justice filed a complaint charging the maintenance of an international cartel in the manufacture and distribution of matches, in violation of the Sherman Antitrust Act, by six American companies, two British companies, a Canadian company, a Swedish company, two American agents of the Swedish company, and six of their officers.

Named as defendants in the suit were: Diamond Match Company, New York City (including William A. Fairburn, President, and Howard F. Holman, Vice-President); Berst-Forster-Dixfield Company, New York City (including Robert G. Fairburn, President); William Gordon Corporation, New York City; Universal Match Corporation, St. Louis, Missouri; Ohio Match Company, New York City; Lion Match Company, Inc., New York City; British Match Corporation, Limited, London, England (including Sir Clarence Bartholomew, Managing Director); Bryant & May, Limited, London, England; Eddy Match Company, Limited, Pembroke, Ontario, Canada; Svenska Tändsticks Aktiebolaget (Swedish Match Company), Jönköpings, Sweden; Transamerican Match Corporation, New York City (including Fritz Otterberg, President); New York Match Co., Inc., New York City, American agents of Swedish Match Company (including Paul Bertil Lind, President).

The Government's complaint made the following charges:

(1) A cartel comprising American, Swedish, British, and Canadian match producers eliminated competition throughout the

world in the manufacture and distribution of matches. This cartel has been in existence since 1901.

(2) The defendants divided world territories into non-competing areas, established production and sales quotas, and restricted the production of matches in the major markets of the world.

(3) The defendants suppressed inventions and improvements in the match art. By the acquisition of patents controlling the "repeating" or "everlasting" match, the defendants have been able virtually to suppress its production and use.

(4) Defendants controlled patents, raw materials, chemicals, machinery, and processes in order to maintain their grip on the industry and prevent competitive capital from entering the market.

(5) The defendants acquired competing match producers and distributors wherever and whenever competition threatened.

(6) The amounts of matches imported into the United States from Sweden, Russia, and Japan have been curtailed and prices have been fixed by agreement with the Diamond Match Company with the approval of the other American defendants. Imports into the United States from Canada, the British Empire, and other markets of the world have been virtually eliminated.

(7) As part of the conspiracy, match factories in the United States have been withdrawn from production and scrapped.

(8) As the result of agreements between the Diamond Match Company and I. G. Farbenindustrie, American production of chlorate of potash, essential to match production and certain types of ammunition, was virtually halted during the period between the first World War and the second World War. This conspiracy resulted in a grave shortage of chlorate of potash for military purposes and match production.

(9) Post-war plans have already been made by the defen-

dants to resume the conspiracy in full as soon as the difficulties created by the war disappear.

The conspiracy in the world match industry against which the complaint was directed was reinforced by an agreement entered into in 1920 by Ivar Kreuger, the late so-called "match king," and William Fairburn on behalf of their respective companies, the Swedish Match Company and the Diamond Match Company.

These two companies are the major factors in the match industry of the world. The Swedish Match Company is the world's largest match producer and exporter. The Diamond Match Company is the largest American match producer. Diamond, through its President, William A. Fairburn, and his personal holding company, the William Gordon Corporation, dominates and controls the policies of Diamond's partly-owned and affiliated company, Berst-Forster-Dixfield Company, and the Universal Match Corporation, Ohio Match Company, and Lion Match Company, Inc.; these companies together with Diamond, produce approximately 83 per cent of American matches. The annual sales of matches in the United States are in excess of $40,000,000.

Prior to the first World War, Diamond was the exclusive agent for Swedish Match for the sale in the United States, Canada, Cuba, and Puerto Rico of safety matches, the type most widely used by the armed forces. When Swedish imports to the United States were cut off during the first World War, Diamond, in 1917, erected a large safety match factory at Savannah, Georgia, to supply the urgent needs of the armed forces of the United States and its allies and civilian requirements for this kind of match.

After the first World War, Kreuger threatened vigorous competition with Diamond in the United States. Faced with this threat, Diamond and Swedish Match entered into an arrangement in 1920 described by Diamond's President, William A. Fairburn, as the "peace treaty with the Swedes." Under the "peace treaty" Swedish Match appointed Diamond its exclusive agent in the United States for the sale of Swedish safety matches and agreed to discontinue all other selling agencies and establishments in the United States. In order to assure Swedish Match of its share of the American match market, it is charged, Kreuger and Fairburn entered into a secret agreement which required Diamond to destroy virtually its entire safety match business, including the scrapping of its largest plant at Savannah, Georgia. Swedish Match agreed that it would not otherwise make or sell matches on the North American Continent; Diamond, in turn, agreed not to make or sell matches in countries supplied by Swedish Match.

The understandings reached in 1920 between Diamond and Swedish Match are still in effect, although the limitation of production feature has been temporarily suspended. Upon the outbreak of the present war a match shortage, particularly of the safety match type, resulted in the United States and in certain South and most Central American countries. In accordance with the agreement between the parties the South and Central American markets were Swedish territory. But war conditions have made it impossible for Swedish Match to supply this market. Instead of selling directly in these markets, however, Diamond, through its controlled affiliate, Berst-Forster-Dixfield, supplied Swedish Match with matches for South and Central American countries. The condition for Diamond's policy in thus helping out was expressed to Swedish Match as follows:

"We help you now. You stay out of the United States market after the war."

By 1927 Kreuger became dissatisfied with the share of Swedish Match and its affiliated company, International Match, in the American match market. In violation of the "peace treaty," he planned to erect new match factories and acquire existing concerns in the United States. William A. Fairburn, on behalf of Diamond, successfully appeased Kreuger for the time being by acquiring Ohio Match, then the second largest domestic match producer, and selling Kreuger a half interest in the company. By 1931 Kreuger, through an arrangement with Fairburn, acquired a one-third interest in Diamond itself. At the same time, Fairburn induced Kreuger to scrap a partly-constructed match factory at Natchez, Mississippi.

In 1901, the complaint charges, Diamond and Bryant & May, virtually the sole match producer in Great Britain, came to an understanding for the elimination of competition between them. Thereafter Bryant & May refrained from producing and selling matches in the United States, and Diamond in the British Empire. It is also charged that the Berst-Forster-Dixfield, Universal, Ohio, and Lion companies have followed Diamond's policies with regard to non-competitive relations with Swedish Match, Bryant & May, and the other corporate defendants.

About 1927 Bryant & May and Swedish Match eliminated competition in the British home market (the United Kingdom and Ireland) and the remainder of the British Empire. Fifty-five per cent of the match consumption of the United Kingdom and Ireland was allotted by Bryant & May's domestic production; the remaining 45 per cent was allotted to Swedish Match's imports. India was allocated to Swedish Match and the remainder of the British Empire to Bryant & May. To effectuate the division of markets, British Match Corporation was formed in 1927 as a holding company, and acquired all of the stock of Bryant & May. Swedish Match obtained 30 per cent of the stock of British Match.

In 1927, it is asserted, Diamond, Bryant & May, and Swedish Match eliminated competition in Canada by the formation of Eddy Match, which acquired virtually all of the match factories in that country.

In 1935, after consultation with and approval by Diamond, Swedish Match, by agreement with the Japanese producers and the Soviet Match Monopoly, fixed the price of and limited match imports into the United States from Japan and Soviet Russia. In about 1937 Diamond became the exclusive agent for all Russian and Japanese matches sold in the United States.

The complaint alleges that about 1922 Diamond's wholly-owned subsidiary, Uniform Chemical Products, became exclusive agent in the United States for the sale of I. G. Farbenindustrie's German-made chlorate of potash. Chlorate of potash is a chemical not only essential in match manufacture, but also in the production of ammunition, flares, and railway emergency warning signals. In return for Uniform's exclusive agency, I. G. Farbenindustrie required Diamond virtually to cease the manufacture of chlorate of potash in the United States. As a result of the scrapping of American plants, this country had practically no plant capacity for the production of chlorate of potash at the outbreak of the war. Emergency plant construction has not yet overcome the shortage of this essential chemical.

The complaint recites the heretofore undisclosed history of the so-called "everlasting" match, which has long been a matter of considerable rumor and speculation. About 1932, it is charged, Kreuger obtained control of the patents on this match, and subsequently Bryant & May obtained an interest in them. Diamond later was offered a participation in Swedish Match's patents and also negotiated with the inventor of certain improvements. Although it was commercially successful in Holland and Switzerland, the everlasting match has never been manufactured commercially by Diamond or any other American manufacturer. Diamond's decision not to acquire the patents and manufacture the everlasting match was expressed as follows in a document found in their files: "The patents have not so long to run and if it becomes a marketable commodity by our pushing it, once the patents are out—as in the case of book-matches—it would be a fertile field for the rottenest kind of competition. It is to be hope that if the item is not put out and pushed by a strong manufacturer, no one else will take it up even if the patents expire."

The Government sought, among other things, the abrogation of the illegal contracts and agreements and a perpetual injunction against the defendants, prohibiting them from violating the Sherman Antitrust Act. The Government also asked that Diamond, Berst-Forster-Dixfield, and the William Gordon Corporation be required to divest themselves of holdings in any other match producer, including the foreign corporate defendants.

12
The Webb Act

An expanding foreign trade is one of our chief economic objectives. Both Government and business should desire and promote policies that will open up new markets to American enterprise, encourage sound foreign investment and facilitate the flow of goods between this and other countries. There can be no issue, surely, over this basic purpose. Nor is there room for disagreement on the proposition that a crucial, if not indeed the ultimate, test of our economic policy should be its efficacy in promoting free enterprise as opposed to a controlled economy. Differences, if any, relate only to methods.

However, anyone who has been under the impression that the Webb Act provides an easy backdoor entrance for American firms to join forces with cartels seeking domination and control of world markets is in for sad disillusionment. The Webb Act was intended to strengthen American competition against foreign cartels. It was enacted by Congress in the belief that it would provide a means of assistance to American business in combatting the power of foreign cartels dominating world markets. The Act was not passed to permit American firms to take part in cartel restrictions on American trade—such restrictions are directly contrary to Congressional purpose.

It should be emphasized that associations organized under the Webb Act cannot legally enter into international agreements which restrict production and distribution, divide territories and fields of operation, fix prices or otherwise regiment industry throughout the world. Neither can they legally enter into agreements which restrain trade within the United States, restrain the export trade of any domestic competitor or association, or which enhance or depress prices or substantially lessen competition within the United States.

We have instituted a suit against the United States Alkali Export Association, the California Alkali Export Association and others, charging them with maintaining international cartel agreements to restrain trade in the manufacture and distribution of alkalis in violation of the Sherman Act. In this case we have charged that activities by the defendants were not authorized by the Webb Act. I shall refer later to this case in more detail. It is sufficient to say at this point that other associations are under investigation for similar activity, and that new antitrust suits will be instituted whenever evidence discloses illegal activity by export associations or others.

The alkali suit may very well have prompted the resolution of the Board of Directors of the the Commerce and Industry Association of New York to declare that Congress should restudy the Webb Act and by proper amendments bring it up to date so that there can be achieved under it all of the objectives that President Wilson sought to attain when he procured the enactment of this Act in 1918. The resolution recited that the Department of Justice program for enforcement of the Sherman Act seemed to be seeking to impose the competitive system and the antitrust philosophy, as interpreted by the United States Supreme Court, on other countries, and implied that antitrust enforcement was frustrating the purposes of the Webb Act.

And in other quarters it has been suggested that perhaps the Webb Act provides a vehicle for attaining cartel objectives without incurring the penalties of the Sherman Act.

These suggestions that the enforcement of the Sherman Act in the field of foreign trade somehow constitutes a betrayal of the Congressional policy embodied in the Webb Act, and that the Webb Act legalizes restrictive cartel practices, are based upon a misconception of the meaning and purpose of the Act. The Webb Act was enacted to help American business compete with foreign cartels. It was not passed to provide a conduit for joining them. It was designed to stimulate the position of American concerns as competitors for world trade and to stimulate the growth of our export trade. The Act created only a very limited exemption from the Sherman Act which I shall presently discuss.

But, before taking up the Act itself, let us look at the conditions which brought about its enactment. The background of the Act is set forth extensively in a report by the Federal Trade Commission, dated June 30, 1916, on cooperation in American export trade. This report set forth that other nations had certain advantages in foreign trade because of superior facilities and more effective organizations; it pointed out that doubt and fear as to legal restrictions prevented Americans from developing effective organizations for engaging in international trade, and that as a result the smaller concerns suffered because of their lack of organization and facilities. It emphasized that in seeking business abroad, American manufacturers and producers had to meet aggressive competition from powerful foreign combinations often international in character. It recited that in some industries the smaller manufacturers had to compete abroad with great American companies having much more efficient worldwide selling organizations. In order to assist these smaller businesses to acquire proper facilities for doing an international business, and to enable them to meet the competition in prices and services of major American concerns and all foreign competitors, the report recommended that small American producers and manufacturers should be permitted to unite their efforts for purposes of conducting foreign trade. By combining their efforts it was thought that these small firms would be better able to advertise, maintain an adequate selling force, and create markets abroad.

But, while recognizing the desirability of a certain degree of cooperation in seeking international markets, the Federal Trade Commission in its 1916 report was fully cognizant of the possibility of misuse of export associations and of the necessity to prevent their misuse by legislative safeguards and antitrust enforcement. Thus the Commission said:

"Two chief dangers from cooperation export organizations of American manufacturers and producers are apparent. They may be used to exploit the home market and they may be used unfairly against individual American exporters in foreign trade. The dangers in cooperative action must be faced frankly and provided against fully.

"The Commission is confident that this can be done without sacrificing the essential advantages of joint action and without altering the policy of the antitrust laws or interfering with their enforcement."

And the Commission further declared that "This recommendation is made subject to the condition that the legislation shall be carefully safeguarded and shall make absolutely clear that the combinations for export business are subject to all of the rigors of the Sherman law if they are used to restrain trade in the United States."

Bills were then introduced in Congress by Senator Pomerene

and Congressman Webb, and were considered by Congressional committees and debated from 1916 to 1918, when the law was enacted. The Webb Act as finally passed provides that nothing in the Sherman Act shall be construed as declaring to be illegal an export association or any agreement made or act done in the course of export trade by such association, provided that such association, agreement or act does not: (a) restrain trade within the United States; or (b) restrain the export trade of any domestic competitor or association; or (c) enhance or depress prices within the United States, substantially lessen competition within the United States, or otherwise restrain trade therein.

Since the Webb Act is a statute creating an exception to the Sherman Act's general application, the principle of interpretation governing all statutes which create such exceptions must be applied here; that is, the Webb Act must be strictly construed. It must not be taken to cover any more ground than appears to have been intended by the language of the Act itself read in the light of the legislative history.

The legislative history leaves no doubt whatever as to what Congress intended. In its report of May 11, 1917, the House Judiciary Committee stated:

"The bill is drawn so as to leave in full force our antitrust laws as applied to our own markets and as affecting different American exporters in their dealings with each other. . . . The bill does not authorize any violation of the present antitrust laws. . . . The bill prohibits the slightest violation of our antitrust laws within the United States."

The Senate Committee report contained a similar declaration.

The House and Senate debates abound with declarations by the sponsors of the bill that it did not in any way interfere with the application of the Sherman Act to the domestic commerce of the United States and to agreements to restrain the export trade of competitors of the associations. In referring to antitrust jurisdiction over proposed export associations, Representative Webb stated: "If the combination for export trade affects unduly or artificially the prices in the United States then they come within the Sherman Antitrust Law."

Senator Pomerene made the following significant arguments during debate on the bill:

"The position was taken in substance that this bill was a repeal of the Sherman Antitrust Law, and if it became the law of the land and these associations were authorized they would at once seek to control the foreign market and probably enter into a combination with foreign companies and cartels engaged in the same line of business and thus reenforced and worldwide in their control of products they would reduce the prices of food animals, of grain, and of other products and raise the prices to the consumer when it suited their purposes."

"If the Senator when making this argument had recited facts instead of fancies, there might have been some force in his utterances but he was giving free reign to his imagination. The Senator overlooked the fact that this bill does not repeal the Sherman Law. He had in mind one paragraph only and lost sight of all the restrictions and qualifications it contains. I submit that when this bill is construed judicially it will be analyzed as a whole and not one part separate from the other.

"The Senator forgets that neither the associations, nor their agreements, nor their actions can be in restraint of trade within the United States, nor in restraint of the foreign trade of any domestic competitor and they cannot by any agreement, conspiracy, or act artificially or intentionally and unduly either enhance prices or reduce prices domestically, and if they do they violate the law of the land."

During the debates some members of Congress, foreseeing

the possibility that export associations might join in a combination with foreign companies, questioned the sponsors of the bill as to the effect of the bill upon such practices. In the House debates, Mr. Moore of Pennsylvania asked: "Suppose a combination in which Americans join with foreigners had been formed?" To this query Congressman Webb replied: "Then you violate the antitrust law and it has been so held by the court." Later, in the Senate debates, Senator Pomerene stated: "There is nothing in this bill authorizing the division of territory abroad."

Attempts to amend the Act between 1921 and 1928 failed. Amendments proposed in 1928 would have extended the Act to include combinations for importation of crude rubber, potash, sisal and other raw materials not made, produced, or grown in substantial quantities within the United States. The bill proposed that year was stated by the House Judiciary Committee to be designed "to meet an acute situation affecting the import trade of the country" by reason of the fact that certain foreign governments controlled and operated monopolies dealing in rubber, potash and sisal for which this country depended materially upon importations. Because of the operation of these foreign monopolies the price to American importers had been greatly increased. The Committee thought that the best way of meeting "these alien government combinations" was to allow American buyers of the monopolized products to combine for the purpose of importing them. During debates on the bill it was attacked, among other things, on the ground that if it were passed, import associations would be permitted to join with foreign producers in worldwide agreements arranging world markets and fixing world prices. The bill failed to pass, Congress thus indicating its unwillingness to extend further the application of the Webb Act.

Thus it is clear that from the very beginning of the agitation for the Act it was understood that the activities of export associations would have to be strictly limited to the promotion of foreign export trade, and that any agreements or activities which restrain domestic competitors either in domestic or foreign commerce would still be illegal under the Sherman Act. This, it seems to me, is what has been overlooked by those who now question the application of the Sherman Act to activities of export associations which restrain domestic competition and the export trade of competitors.

The Department of Justice is not seeking any novel interpretation of the Sherman Act or of the Webb Act. We have thus far instituted one suit involving associations formed under the Webb Act and it requires no novel interpretation of the Act to sustain the allegations involved.

In that suit, filed on March 16, 1944, we charged two American export associations, 13 American manufacturers, and a British corporation and its American agent, with maintaining international cartel agreements to restrain trade in the manufacture and marketing of *alkalis*, in violation of the Sherman Antitrust Act. Our complaint asserted that the 17 defendants and four co-conspirators—two American corporations, one German, and one Belgian—had conspired to allocate and maintain exclusive marketing areas and export quotas throughout the world, eliminating competition and restraining exports in alkalis by means of illegal contracts, agreements and understandings still in effect!

The following were named as defendants in the complaint: United States Alkali Export Association, Inc. ("Alkasso"), a Delaware corporation with principal offices in New York City; California Alkali Export Association ("Calkex"), a California corporation with principal offices in Los Angeles; Imperial

Chemical Industries Ltd. ("ICI"), a British corporation with principal offices in London, England; Imperial Chemical Industries (New York) Ltd., a New York corporation wholly owned and controlled by ICI, London; Pittsburgh Plate Glass Company, Inc., a Pennsylvania corporation with principal offices in New York City; Church & Dwight Company, Inc., a Delaware corporation with principal offices in New York City; Diamond Alkali Company, Inc., a Delaware corporation with principal offices in Pittsburgh, Pa.; Dow Chemical Company, Inc., a Michigan corporation with principal offices in Midland, Mich.; Hooker Electrochemical Company, Inc., a New York corporation with principal offices in Niagara Falls, N. Y.; The Mathieson Alkali Works, Inc., a Virginia corporation with principal offices in New York City; Niagara Alkali Company, a New York corporation with principal offices in New York City; Pennsylvania Salt Manufacturing Company, a Pennsylvania corporation with principal offices in Philadelphia; Southern Alkali Corporation, a Delaware corporation with principal offices in New York City; Westvaco Chlorine Products Corporation, a Delaware corporation with principal offices in New York City; Wyandotte Chemicals Corporation, a Michigan corporation with principal offices in Detroit; West End Chemical Company, Inc., a California corporation with principal offices in Oakland; and Pacific Alkali Company, Inc., a limited partnership organized and registered in California with principal offices in Los Angeles. Named as co-conspirators were: American Potash & Chemical Corporation, a Delaware corporation with principal offices in New York City, substantially all of whose capital stock beneficially owned by the German potash trust, was seized by the Alien Property Custodian in 1942; Solvay Process Company, a New York corporation with principal offices in New York City; Solvay et Cie. ("Belgian Solvay"), a Belgian corporation with principal offices formerly in Brussels but now in London, England; and I. G. Farbenindustrie Aktiengesellschaft, a German corporation with headquarters in Frankfort-am-Main, Germany.

This suit is of major importance in the drive to eliminate the effect of cartels on American commerce. It is the first suit which the Antitrust Division has filed involving the activities of associations organized under the Webb Export Trade Act. It should serve as a warning of our determination to prevent cartel groups from carrying out their illegal plans by use of the Webb Act.

"Alkalis," it should be explained, include soda ash (sodium carbonate), caustic soda (sodium hydroxide) and bicarbonate of soda. Soda ash is used in the manufacture of glass, textiles and chemicals. Caustic soda is used in the manufacture of soap, textiles, rayon and paper and in the refining of petroleum products. Sodium bicarbonate is used for many industrial, chemical and drug purposes and, purified, as baking soda. In 1939, there were produced in the United States approximately 2,900,000 tons of soda ash, worth more than $50,000,000; approximately 1,000,000 tons of caustic soda, worth more than $40,000,000; and approximately 140,000 tons of refined bicarbonate of soda, worth more than $5,000,000.

All the domestic defendants in the suit, with the exception of Alkasso, Calkex and ICI (N. Y.), were engaged in the manufacture and sale of alkalis in the United States and conduct substantially all of their export trade in alkalis through Alkasso and Calkex. Alkasso was organized in 1919 and filed a verified statement with the Federal Trade Commission to obtain benefits and immunities provided by the Webb Export Trade Act. Alkasso's members, who control and manage all its activities, include defendants Pennsylvania Salt, Pittsburgh Plate Glass,

Hooker Electrochemical, Diamond, Mathieson, Westvaco, Church & Dwight, Dow, Niagara and Southern. Alkasso obtains alkalis from its members, transporting from warehouses maintained at Hoboken, N. J., and New Orleans, La., to markets throughout the world. Calkex was organized similarly in 1936 by American Potash & Chemical, West End Chemical and Pacific Alkali, who control and manage its activities. It obtains alkalis from member companies and ships from Pacific Coast ports to various world markets. Prior to 1940, Alkasso and Calkex together exported 95% of the alkalis exported from the United States. Since then, because of war conditions and the resignation of Solvay from Alkasso in 1941, the alkalis exported by the two associations have amounted to 75% of the total alkali exports from the U. S.

It is charged that beginning in 1924 and continuing to the present day the defendants have engaged in an unlawful combination and conspiracy in restraint of trade and commerce in alkalis and that they have been and are parties to contracts, agreements and understandings in violation of the Sherman Act. This continuing agreement, it is alleged, provides:

(1) That Alkasso, Calkex, their respective members, ICI, I. G. Farben, and Belgian Solvay not compete with each other in the sale of alkalis in any market of the world outside of the United States, and that ICI, I. G. Farben and Belgian Solvay refrain from importing alkalis into the United States;

(2) That Alkasso, Calkex and their respective members be assigned certain marketing areas as their exclusive territory (including the U. S.) and that ICI, I. G. Farben and Belgian Solvay refrain from exporting alkalis to such territory and prevent other European manufacturers from doing so;

(3) That exclusive market areas be assigned to ICI (the

British Empire exclusive of Canada), I. G. Farben (Scandinavia), and Belgian Solvay (Continental Europe exclusive of the Scandinavian countries), and that Alkasso and Calkex and their respective members refrain from exporting alkalis to such territories and prevent other American manufacturers from doing so.

(4) That the rest of the world markets be shared jointly by Alkasso, Calkex, their respective members, and ICI, with competition therein eliminated by allocating quotas to British and American companies and limiting their exports to certain fixed percentages of the total sold in such areas and by agreeing among themselves on the prices at which alkalis are sold in such markets;

(5) That Alkasso, Calkex and their respective members prevent other American manufacturers and dealers from exporting to joint territory except in compliance with quota and price agreements fixed for such markets.

(6) That Alkasso, Calkex, and their respective members conduct their export trade and utilize the aforesaid arrangements and their practices thereunder in such manner as to enhance, stabilize and maintain at uniform and non-competitive levels the prices at which caustic soda is sold in the United States.

It is alleged that the results of this conspiracy have been:

(1) To eliminate competition by Alkasso, Calkex and their members with ICI and European producers of alkalis in the manufacture and marketing of alkalis throughout the world;

(2) To eliminate exports of alkalis by ICI, Belgian Solvay and I. G. Farben to the United States;

(3) To eliminate exports of alkalis by Alkasso, Calkex and other American manufacturers to many markets of the world;

and to restrict and curtail by quota arrangements the export of alkalis from the United States to many world markets;

(4) To eliminate competition by Alkasso and its members with Calkex and its members in exports of alkalis from the United States;

(5) To curtail and limit the production of alkalis within the United States;

(6) To prevent competition between manufacturers of alkalis in the United States (who are not members of Alkasso and Calkex) and Alkasso, Calkex, ICI, Belgian Solvay and I. G. Farben in world markets;

(7) To prevent independent exporters of alkalis in the United States from engaging in the export of such commodities; and

(8) To enhance, stabilize and maintain at arbitrary price levels the prices at which caustic soda is sold in the United States.

The Department of Justice sought the abrogation of the illegal contracts and agreements and a permanent injunction against the defendants restraining them from violating the Sherman Act. The Government also asked that the defendants be enjoined from entering into any future contract, agreement or understanding with any foreign company in any manner restricting their exports of alkalis from the United States by division of export markets, allocation of territories, fixing of prices in export sales, or fixing or observing any export quotas. The Government further asked that the domestic defendants be enjoined from selling alkalis exported from the United States in any foreign markets through ICI (N. Y.) or through any agent or dealer selling alkalis for or on behalf of ICI or ICI (N. Y.).

Thus, in this case, we allege a conspiracy to restrain the exports of American competitors; to restrict imports to the United

States and thereby restrain trade within the United States; to curtail and limit production in the United States, and to enhance, stabilize and maintain price levels within the United States. These allegations clearly charge a violation of the Sherman Act. The Webb Act, I am confident, does not protect activities of this type.

The allegations in this single instance against a Webb Export Association raise serious questions of law violation which cannot be ignored. The suggestion that we are stretching the Sherman Act by novel interpretation simply does not stand up. Associations organized under the Webb Act should take warning that the Alkali case represents the view of the Department of Justice as to the application of the Sherman Act to the activities of such associations. The position of the Department is in accord with the purpose, history and language of the Webb Act.

It is the policy of the Department of Justice to enforce the Sherman Act as vigorously as possible whenever evidence establishes probable violation. The Sherman Act represents a Congressional policy of more than fifty years' standing. The Department of Justice did not create the Act although it has the responsibility of making it effective. The Department of Justice does not interpret the Act. That is the task of the courts. It is true, however, that the attitude of the Department of Justice toward antitrust law enforcement is predicated, frankly, not on a passive interest in the matter—a grudging willingness to perform an unwelcome duty—but on a deep conviction that Congress is right, and that the public economic policy embodied in the Sherman Act is basically sound.

So long as the conditions which gave rise to the Webb Act still exist, the Act, if properly employed, may be useful in promoting trade within the special and limited domain to which the Act applies. To meet centralized buying by centralized selling, and to stand up against the exclusionary tactics and monopolistic practices of well-established foreign cartels is sometimes necessary. Joint action by American exporters may serve to secure an equal footing in foreign trade in markets where combination is permitted or even encouraged. No doubt such retaliatory measures are wasteful as ways of organizing world trade, and no doubt we and other nations would be better advised to join hands in getting rid of international trade restraints, theirs and our alike. Meanwhile, however, the Webb Act has a use in defending American interests in markets which are too often cartelized.

If export associations are to be economically useful in the postwar world, approved by public policy and serving the purpose for which they were created, they must be the spearhead of American industry as it enters into competition with foreign industry for a fair share of world markets, rather than the tool of international monopolists to draw American industries into restrictive cartel agreements which contain provisions in conflict with the Sherman Act.

I have given some thought to the question whether the Webb Act should be tightened—whether additional legislation should be enacted to assure that possible abuses shall be eradicated. Some of those who have suggested such legislation apparently feel that export associations, operating under the cloak of the Webb Act, may be used to carry American industries into private international cartels which operate contrary to our public policy, and that serious consideration should be given now to legislation that would make such abuses impossible.

But at present, I am not ready to believe that additional legislation is necessary. Vigilant enforcement of the Sherman Act against those who misuse the Webb Act together with the understanding and cooperation of industry will make additional legislation unnecessary and prove adequate to prevent export associations from becoming screens for illegal cartel activity. The appreciation by industry itself of the advantage of avoiding restrictive agreements is an important factor in our future policy. But if antitrust enforcement should prove ineffectual, and if the postwar period should be characterized by widespread misuse of export associations operating under the cloak of the Webb Act, then, of course, serious consideration will have to be given to legislation which will end the abuses.

13

Private Governments

One of the foremost problems facing our government today is the formulation of an economic policy for the future. The development of this policy is the concern of every American and will affect vitally (1) the domestic prosperity of this country, (2) our role in world affairs, (3) our national security. I should like to point out in this connection certain important considerations which must be taken into account if errors of the past are to be avoided and progress in the future guaranteed.

No economic policy adopted by the government can be effective if the industrial policies of the country in the international field are determined, controlled, and executed by private agreements of which the government has no knowledge. The formulation and conduct of the foreign policy of the United States is provided for in the Constitution: "[The President] shall have Power, by and with the Advice and Consent of the Senate, to make Treaties, provided two thirds of the Senators present concur."

Past history demonstrates clearly that our economic foreign policy has in many instances been rendered ineffectual by the operation of secret agreements conceived and ratified by cartels.

These agreements admit of no sovereignty other than their own, and serve no interests other than the shortsighted aims of monopoly. This has only too often resulted in situations which have endangered our national security, injured our position in the world economy, and denied us opportunity for the fullest use of our resources and labor. Domestically, businessmen have had to yield to the dictates of large aggregates of power vested in international cartels. What and how much they might produce, and to whom and at what price they might sell, have been decided for them. If they did not yield, they risked elimination.

Internationally, our foreign policy has in many respects been frustrated. The Good Neighbor policy governing our relations with Latin America, the reciprocal trade treaties, our alien property policy, and other basic principles of America's conduct of foreign affairs have in many instances been seriously weakened by the interference of cartel activities. Indeed, it is difficult to see how our future policies—for example the Atlantic Charter—can be executed successfully, if the dispositions made by cartels continue into the postwar world.

Cartels will find it difficult to operate if the agreements upon which they are based are open to public scrutiny and examination. Any law requiring the filing of international agreements should operate like the Foreign Agents' Registration Act. It should not give immunity to cartels, but should let the government and the public know of their existence, their identity, and their scope.

The cost of secrecy is illustrated by the following examples. Two very basic raw materials necessary to any industrial community are petroleum and rubber. The crucial nature of these materials to our industrial economy and military operations is clearly apparent. Without them, practically all industrial activity would cease. Yet our oil and rubber supplies have been dependent upon policies arrived at secretly, operated clandestinely, and run in a manner contrary to the fundamental foreign policy of our country. The public had no voice in making these private policies, yet today it bears the burden of their effects.

The very nature of modern warfare and industrial life is such that both petroleum and rubber have political and military, as well as economic, aspects. Not all countries have petroleum within their borders and, prior to the present war, only Britain, for practical purposes, had rubber. Access to these raw materials is a prime military requisite to any nation desirous of maintaining a strong international position. Without them, no nation could hope to wage a war, maintain a healthy industrial economy, or impose a treaty of Munich.

Among Germany's raw material deficiencies, oil and rubber have been the two greatest. Within her own borders there is little, if any, oil, and no rubber. This fact has certainly been a consideration in the basis of our own as well as the French and British foreign policy. Hence, the discovery in 1926 that petroleum could be made from Germany's plentiful coal was a political event of the first magnitude. That synthetic rubber became a reality in Germany shortly afterward served to magnify the shock.

The petroleum industry, dominated in this country by Standard Oil Co. (New Jersey), was shaken at its very foundation. A Standard Oil official, Frank Howard, wrote at the time from Mannheim, Germany, on March 28, 1926, to Walter Teagle, president of Standard Oil, the following:

"Based upon my observations and discussion today, I think that this matter is the most important which has ever faced the company since the dissolution.

"The Badische can make high grade motor fuel from lignite and other low quality coals in amounts up to half the weight of the coal. This means absolutely the independence of Europe on the matter of gasoline supply. Straight price competition is all that is left. . . .

"They can make up to 100% by weight from any liquid hydrocarbon, tar, fuel oil, or crude oil. This means that refining of oil will have as a competitive industry in America and elsewhere, catalytic conversion of the crude into motor fuel.

. . . .

"I shall not attempt to cover any details, but I think this will be evidence of my state of mind"

Standard Oil was worried about its monopoly position. The discovery threatened competition and Standard Oil met the threat.

The process of making oil from coal was controlled by I. G. Farbenindustrie, the German chemical trust. In 1926 a meeting between Standard Oil and I. G. Farben was arranged. The result was a series of treaties. The agreements preserved the position of the parties in the fields which they respectively dominated. As stated by a Standard Oil official: "The I. G. are going to stay out of the oil business proposition and we are going to stay out of the chemical business insofar as that has no bearing on the oil business."

Competition between I. G. Farben and Standard Oil was eliminated, and the technology of chemistry and petroleum was was made part of their feudal preserve. The economic effect was the maintenance of monopoly.

Stated in a more detailed way, Standard Oil was given the world right on the oil process and I. G. Farben was given the chemical business of the world. But there was one exception.

While I. G. was given the right to engage in the oil business in Germany, Standard Oil was permitted to engage in the chemical business in the United States only as a junior partner to I. G. The staggering implications of this are clear. Germany could not afford, considering her aims, to permit any outsider to control within her own borders as important a development to her national life as the production of oil from coal.

But when Standard Oil gave up its rights in the chemical field, including those in the United States, the repercussions were to seriously affect our wartime efforts.

Included in the chemical field was the synthetic rubber, buna. Under the agreements, therefore, it was a German-controlled monopoly. When the war broke out in September 1939, the Germans had not permitted buna to be manufactured in the United States. We had no experience, information, or know-how, and we had not obtained permission from Germany to produce synthetic rubber. Of equal importance is the fact that the United States Government had no knowledge of these facts. The terms of the Standard Oil-I. G. Farben treaty were secret.

When corporations outside the I. G.-Standard Oil orbit attempted to manufacture buna rubber, they were confronted with the combined strength, wealth and power of the private coalition. Goodrich and Goodyear attempted such production, but the former was sued for patent infringement and the latter formally threatened with suit by the Standard Oil Company under the I. G. patents. This took place in October 1941, a few weeks before Pearl Harbor. Thus, not only did Standard Oil agree with I. G. Farben that the latter should control the exploitation of synthetic rubber, but cooperated in preventing anyone else from producing. In fact, on April 20, 1938, a Standard Oil official wrote as follows:

"Until we have this permission, however, there is absolutely nothing we can do and we must be especially careful not to make any move whatever even on a purely informal, personal or friendly basis, without the consent of our friends. We know some of the difficulties they have, both from business complications and interrelations with the rubber and chemical trades in the United States, and from a national standpoint in Germany, but we do not know the whole situation—and since under the agreement they have full control over the exploitation of this process, the only thing we can do is to continue to press for authority to act, but in the meantime loyally preserve the restrictions they have put on us."

On its own, Standard Oil received little, if any, information on synthetic rubber from I. G. The following quotations from Standard Oil letters and documents are clear:

"Our people have never made buna . . . the I. G. has not furnished anyone technical information."

"The only information our people have is derived from published patents."

"Information . . . about the technical aspects of this development has not been forthcoming as a result of the German Government's refusal because of military expediency to permit I. G. to reveal such information to anyone outside Germany."

The ambiguous position in which Standard found itself arises from the fact that Standard never considered that it was making foreign policy, or took into account the political implications of its acts. We neither expect nor require this of our businessmen. After all, they are not supposed to have such responsibility. Nevertheless, neither Standard Oil nor the country could escape the consequences of these agreements. It would seem, in the light of this experience, that the least the Government can do is to provide a mechanism for acquainting itself with the existence and terms of such agreements. The Government, on the other hand, is unable to make proper judgments if it does not have complete information.

The Monroe Doctrine and the Good Neighbor policy are both pillars of our foreign relations. Nevertheless, many cartel agreements ran directly counter to these policies. The causes of conflict are not difficult to understand. In a large number of cartel agreements, world territory is divided into exclusive, noncompetitive domains. In the drug, magnesium, optical glass, dyestuffs, plastics and a host of fields, the United States was the exclusive territory of American cartel members. The rest of the world was allocated to Germany. This included Latin America. As a result, the Germans were able to set up economic colonies in Latin America and elsewhere free from American competition. The large numbers of Nazis in South America were a partial consequence of the character of these agreements.

When the Nazis came to power in Germany, they immediately utilized the cartel system as a device for political, as well as economic, infiltration in countries outside of Germany, particularly in the Western Hemisphere. A bold assertion of this policy is set forth in a communication, written in 1933, from a director of Robert Bosch, A. G., of Germany, to the president of the United American Bosch Corporation, which states:

"With regard to the political situation . . . only one thing is very evident, namely, that all forces of administrative and economic endeavour such as the different cartels, etc., are to be brought into one definite line of endeavour coinciding, of course, with the policy of the ruling [Nazi] party and that individual opinions and utterances will be submitted to a similar rule."

When the present war broke out, Germany, because of the sea blockade, was unable to supply goods to Latin America. Cartels made full provision for the contingency of war. The South American market was preserved for the German firms by cartel members of other countries, notably the United States. Not only did American cartel members supply products to the German agents in South America, in many cases they used German labels. What is most important, they agreed to withdraw at the end of the war and once again give Germany a free hand in Latin America. In some cases, realizing that the blacklist might make this kind of arrangement difficult, dummy firms in South America stood ready to replace those blacklisted. Many instances of efforts by cartels to maintain their usual relations, and to preserve the restrictions by which German dominance in South American markets was achieved, are available. A characteristic attitude is indicated in the statement made by the head of the Chemical Marketing Co., an American firm, which had relations with the Deutsche Gold-und-Silber Scheideanstalt of Germany. In the early period of the war, this officer of the American company wrote:

"We insure thereby that the German trade up to the present with our South and Central American friends can be held firmly in our hands and, should export from Germany become impossible—as you yourself can well visualize—the loss would be much less if for the duration of the war American chemicals can be delivered, rather than complete loss of business for many, many years, if we place our clients in such a position that they can continue to serve their customers."

The dyestuffs industry ranks among the most strategic branches of production. During the first World War, the United States and the Allies experienced severe and crippling shortages of dyestuffs, medicines and related products which were controlled by the German dyestuffs cartel. In the years between the Armistice in 1919 and the outbreak of the present war in 1939, the United States endeavored to build up a strong dyestuffs industry because of its peacetime as well as its wartime importance. The German dye trust, however, succeeded in re-establishing a substantial and significant degree of control in this industry through a series of cartel agreements. In addition, I. G. Farben, through its American subsidiary, General Aniline & Film, was able to exert direct influence on the dyestuffs market in the United States. In the many agreements made between American, British and German dyestuffs producers, the American companies were generally restricted to the domestic markets.

Upon the outbreak of war, when the British blockade threatened to cut off the exports of I. G., it nevertheless attempted to insure the maintenance of its control over various markets. The boldness of I. G.'s tactics is indicated in a cable addressed to General Aniline & Film on September 19, 1939, which released that firm from export restrictions for the purpose of supplying I. G.'s customers and agents in the British Empire. This communication stated:

"In addition to Canada we release you from export restriction in regard to the following countries: Great Britain, British India, Australia, New Zealand but only for duration of present state of war and as far as supplies to following firms are concerned." [A list of distributing agents within the British Empire is included.]

This cable was modified on September 21, 1939, when I. G. communicated further with General Aniline & Film, stating: "Replace in first telegram 'for duration of present state of war' by 'until further notice' and act accordingly." Similar arrangements were made regarding I. G.'s distributing agencies in South America. This effort on I. G.'s part to circumvent the British blockade is further illustration of the implications which inhere in such cartel arrangements.

The same type of practice was no less significant in other

parts of the world. In the winter of 1941, while Congress was debating the Lend-Lease Act, cartel agreements had already decreed that certain critical types of products could not be sold to Great Britain. For example, when Great Britain attempted to place an order for tetrazene-primed ammunition, a cartel agreement between du Pont and I. G. Farben forbade their sale, and it was not made.

In this case the patent attorney for the Remington Arms Company, a subsidiary of du Pont, wrote a memorandum dated January 23, 1941, stating:

"The further sale of Tetrazene Primed Ammunition to the British Purchasing Commission or to the Government of the Union of South Africa or to the Government of Canada is most undesirable by reason of our Tetrazene contract with R. W. S. [Rheinische Westfalische Sprengstoff, a wholly-owned subsidiary of I. G. Farben].

"Article III, Paragraph D of the original contract of November 14, 1929, reads as follows: 'Remington shall not sell military ammunition containing any Tetrazene in Germany and in any or all of the countries in the British Empire.'

. . . . .

"There can be little if any question that pistol and revolver ammunition sold at this time to his Majesty's Government in the United Kingdom is military ammunition . . . or that such sale is a sale in a country of the British Empire within the intent of Article III D of the contract.

"We understand that the Process Division have recommended the use of Tetrazene priming in certain ammunition to be sold to the British Purchasing Commission. It appears obvious that this should not be done."

Similar situations existed in aviation precision equipment,

drugs, and chemicals. Thus, I. G. Farben sought to obtain assurances from du Pont that information on certain industrial processes would not be transmitted to the British. On October 4, 1939, I. G. wrote to du Pont, stating:

"You advise us that for the duration of the war, you will not pass the experiences and applications which you receive from one licensee on to another. We thank you for having quickly taken the necessary steps for meeting the altered conditions."

A significant and clear-cut example of the way in which cartel agreements enabled the German Government to influence the policies of American cartel partners of German industry is provided in the case of aviation instruments. In this instance Siemens-Halske, the great German electrical equipment producer, wrote to Bendix Aviation Company on October 25, 1939, as follows:

"Under our agreement your geographical contract territory includes the United States, its territories and Canada. A state of war exists at the present time between Canada and ourselves.

"Notwithstanding the war we are of course willing to live up to the agreement as far as possible. However, we would appreciate receiving your assurance that the records which you will receive from us within the scope of our agreement will not be given to Canada for the duration of the war and that you will supply no instruments, built under a license, if you know that they are destined for our enemies."

An official of Bendix answered:

"As regards the drawings sent over you may rest assured. As regards fabrication . . . we will arrange to the best of our ability to keep within the orbit of domestic use."

One of the most necessary economic measures of war is the seizure of enemy property. Although we have a policy concerning enemy property, the Antitrust Division of the Department of Justice has come across frequent attempts to nullify this policy by private agreement.

In one case, I. G. Farben transferred over 2,000 patents to the Standard Oil Company. While there may be some dispute as to the purpose of the assignment, the fact is clear. The Alien Property Custodian, even though he has vested this property, found himself in litigation as to whether the patents were in fact transferred in a bona fide manner. Taken together with a provision in the Standard Oil-I. G. Farben contract, this instance presents the result of a carefully-conceived and well-developed policy of not only considering the war as an unfortunate interlude, but as a method of defeating public policy. The clause in question provides that even if the agreement should be interfered with by the government of the United States or if, in effect, war should take place between the countries of the respective parties, then at the conclusion of such interruption the parties shall come to a new agreement "in the spirit of the old."

Another phase of the relationships between Standard Oil and I. G. Farben with respect to the eventuality of war between the United States and Germany is indicated in a letter written by the Assistant Comptroller of Standard Oil to one of the directors of the company, on September 8, 1939. The body of this letter deals with the Standard-I. G. Corporation, a joint subsidiary in which Standard Oil owned 80% and I. G. 20%, which had been formed to carry out the purposes of the Standard Oil-I. G. agreements. Standard Oil was considering the purchase of I. G.'s holdings in this subsidiary company. One paragraph in the letter indicates clearly the objective which Standard Oil sought. This paragraph states:

"Of course what we have in mind is protecting this minority interest in the event of war between ourselves and Germany as it would certainly be very undesirable to have this 20% interest in Standard-I. G. passed to an Alien Property Custodian who might sell to an unfriendly interest."

Another case shows how devious and complex cartel schemes can be. Briefly, the Siemens-Halske Company of Germany and the Beryllium Corporation of America entered into an agreement concerning the production and distribution of beryllium alloys which had all the usual characteristics of a cartel, such as the division of world territory, etc.

Before this highly interesting agreement was entered into, however, Siemens-Halske attempted to protect its position by assigning its patents in this field to the Metal & Thermit Company of New York. Actually these patents were held by Metal & Thermit in escrow for the Siemens-Halske Company. For this service, the Metal & Thermit Company received $10,000.

Without such a bill as is now contemplated, no Alien Property Custodian could have known that the above patents were really property of an enemy national. They would have remained concealed in this instance if it had not been for the fortuitous action of an investigation by the Justice Department.

The titanium and optical goods cases previously related are other examples of this practice.

The development of the magnesium industry in the United States provides further illustration of the political effects of cartels in addition to the corrosive effects of monopoly upon industrial expansion. From an international standpoint the cartelization of the magnesium industry prior to the outbreak of the present war also had serious effects. As a consequence of both monopoly and international cartel arrangements in the industry which induced Germany's potential opponents to restrict output, Germany obtained an initial lead in the production of magnesium so great that it remained substantially unchallenged until 1941. According to estimates made by the

U. S. Bureau of Mines, Germany produced 61% of the world's total output of magnesium in 1937. The United States produced 10%. In 1940 Germany was still producing one-half of the world's output while the United States was producing about 14%.

The importance of magnesium is indicated by the uses for which it is employed. In general, its principal consumer is the aircraft industry. Magnesium is used in the construction of aircraft engines, the frames of airplanes, various interior parts, wheels, and other similar portions of aircraft. Magnesium is also employed in the manufacture of incendiary bombs, tracer bullets, and flares.

The two principal producers in this country during the years 1919 to 1927 were the Dow Chemical Company and the American Magnesium Company, a subsidiary of the Aluminum Company of America. In 1927, the American Magnesium Company ceased production, and the Dow Chemical Company thereafter enjoyed a monopoly in the production of magnesium in the United States. The American Magnesium Company by agreement purchased all of its requirements from Dow and constituted Dow's largest customer. In tracing the relationship between Dow, the sole producer of magnesium, and Alcoa, the sole producer of aluminum, during the period in question, it is essential to bear in mind that magnesium is the principal technological rival to aluminum. Nearly all of the functions for which aluminum is employed can also be fulfilled by magnesium with greater efficiency, in many instances, because magnesium is not only one-third lighter than aluminum, but is more readily machined and, when properly alloyed, has greater tensile strength.

In the year 1931, I. G. Farbenindustrie, the principal producer of magnesium in Germany, entered into an agreement with the Aluminum Company of America known as the Alig Agreement. According to the terms of this contract, a joint corporation, the Magnesium Development Company, was formed in which Alcoa and I. G. each held 50% control. The Magnesium Development Company was primarily a patent-holding corporation to which I. G. transferred some patents for the fabrication of magnesium and to which Alcoa contributed process patents. In addition to participating in the Magnesium Development Company, I. G. also obtained a 50% interest in Alcoa's own subsidiary, the American Magnesium Company.

The significance of the arrangements between Alcoa and I. G. was twofold: Alcoa was interested in obtaining a secure foothold in the magnesium industry in order to protect its primary interest in aluminum; I. G. was endeavoring by its usual tactics to extend the sphere of its influence. It is especially significant to note that in the Alig Agreement it was stipulated that any licenses issued by the jointly-owned Magnesium Development Company were to be restricted to the United States. It was also provided that:

"As long as magnesium is produced by any . . . producing company under a license or licenses granted . . . the holders of the I. G. shares in Alig . . . shall have the right to limit the increases in production capacity of every such producing company after the initial contemplated production capacity shall have been reached. The initial contemplated production capacity shall in no case be more than 4,000 tons per annum."

Dow Chemical Company was not a party to the 1931 agreement between Alcoa and I. G. During the period immediately following the Alig Agreement, every effort was made to bring Dow into the cartel picture, with the consequence that, on January 1, 1934, Dow entered into a patent-holding agreement with Magnesium Development Company. In 1933 also Dow and

American Magnesium Company had entered into a five-year purchase contract by which the American Magnesium Company was guaranteed a position as a preferred customer of Dow. In return, Dow's position as the sole producer of magnesium was protected.

In 1934 Dow also entered into a sales contract with I. G. Farben. This contract stated:

"Dow agrees to confine its sales in Europe solely to the I. G., with the exception that it reserves the right to sell the British Maxium or its successors not more than 300,000 pounds (150 tons) per annum at a price not lower than the price quoted to I. G. for the same quantities, plus an extra charge of not less than 4c per pound for I. G.'s larger consumption. Dow further promises to use its best endeavor to keep British Maxium or its successors from reselling magnesium in ingot form and will try to limit its purchases to its own use in fabricating."

During 1934 and 1935 Dow delivered to I. G. (which was, of course, the principal producer of magnesium in the world) more than 3,800,000 pounds of magnesium out of Dow's total production of little more than 4,000,000 pounds. This magnesium was sold to I. G. at a price approximately 30% below the price to Dow's other customers, with the exception of American Magnesium Corporation, which also enjoyed a preferential position. It is interesting to note that, during this same period, the sales manager of Dow Chemical travelled to England and wrote to his home office as follows:

"They [British Maxium] are very much in need of additional magnesium for the balance of 1935, but they understand our position perfectly well and do not blame us at all because we are not in a position to furnish them the metal they want. They were at fault in not getting in touch with us sooner regarding their increased demands. They advised me that they had exported 20 tons of ingot to Europe but I later obtained definite proof from Mr. Ziegler of the I. G. that they had exported 60 tons in Europe. If they had kept this metal in England they would have had sufficient supplies for this year."

It may be remarked that, in consequence of these arrangements between Dow and I. G., I. G.'s position in the European magnesium market was enormously strengthened. One particularly significant result of I. G.'s dominance was that Great Britain was rendered primarily dependent upon Germany for its magnesium imports. As late as 1938, 87.9% of the magnesium imported into Great Britain was obtained from Germany. When war broke out, Great Britain was at once cut off from a large part of its magnesium supply.

From the standpoint of the development of the industry in the United States, it is clear that the total effect of the arrangements among Alcoa, I. G., and Dow was to restrict magnesium production. The extent of the disparity in the magnesium output of Germany and the United States is clearly evident in the production figures for the years 1937 to 1940. In 1940, the year in which France fell, the United States produced 5,680 tons, while Germany produced more than 19,000 tons. Strenuous efforts on the part of the government and industry have been necessary to expand magnesium production sufficiently to meet our minimum wartime needs. The large plant construction undertaken by the government in cooperation with various magnesium producers has achieved initial success. It is clearly evident, however, that the magnesium program had to be inaugurated and carried out under the tremendous handicap of the monopoly situation which existed in the industry prior to the war.

It is equally clear that, from a political standpoint, the government began its operations completely in the dark. It is scarcely credible that, had the arrangements between Alcoa and I. G. and between Dow and I. G. been known to the government at the time at which they were made, the risks inherent in private treaty making of this type would have been permitted to exist.

It is characteristic of many cartel agreements which are arrived at secretly and maintained in silence that concealment of their provisions is motivated by the desire to avoid scrutiny of their operations by public authority. In some instances, the illegal nature of the terms of cartel agreements explains the cloak of secrecy which is cast over their provisions. Moreover, it is often stipulated in cartel agreements that, in the eventuality of action taken by government, the parties to the agreements shall cooperate in order to maintain their relationships despite anything that government may do.

There are numerous examples among the many agreements which have been investigated by the Department of Justice which clearly reveal the intent as well as the necessity for secrecy from the point of view of the cartels. Thus, in a letter from Canadian Industries, Limited, to the du Pont Company, the writer states:

"In the course of recent meetings in connection with the new Patents and Processes Agreement, I understand a suggestion has been made by the du Pont legal representatives which will involve the new agreement making specific reference to the respective territorial rights of du Pont and ICI. I cannot help feeling that on broad grounds this is undesirable both from the viewpoint of C-I-L and of the major stockholders. For instance, should any investigation take place in Canada which will require the production of this agreement, the clause in question would automatically necessitate the production in its term of the ICI and du Pont agreements: at least that is the way we would read it, and this would be bound to lead to publicity of a very undesirable nature in regard to the division of world territories. My practical suggestion is that, as the detailed prior commitments are now to be dealt with in the form of a letter separate from the agreement (this at the suggestion of the du Pont legal representatives) it might be possible to include the point in question in that separate letter also."

The attitude of cartels toward the relation between their own policies and the policies of government are epitomized in the exchange of correspondence between Sir Harry McGowan, Chairman of the Board of Imperial Chemical Industries, and Lammot du Pont in May 1933. Sir Harry wrote:

"With a large organization such as we have I find it is a good thing to issue such warnings from time to time—one went out at the time of the Ottawa Conference—so that everything possible is done to ensure that no prospective political or legislative action on the part of governments is permitted to influence relations between du Pont and I.C.I."

On June 17, 1933, Lammot du Pont replied as follows:

"I am much interested in what you say and have heartily approved your attitude toward our Patents and Processes Agreement and the relations between the two companies. I feel the same; namely that our relations have been so happy and have produced such satisfactory results that we should let nothing in the way of international agreements interfere in any way with the progress we have made or may make in the future. If any legislation or international agreements are brought about which affect these I.C.I.-du Pont relations I am sure we will be able to adjust ourselves so as to get the continued benefit of our agreement."

A striking and instructive illustration of the role of secrecy in cartel agreements is provided in the terms of an arrangement concerning the pharmaceutical industry, between the Schering Corporation of Bloomfield, New Jersey, and the Schering, A. G., of Germany. One clause in this agreement, which was made in 1938, stated that "the existence, the content, and the details of operation of this agreement have to be kept secret by both parties notwithstanding the possible obligation of disclosing it to public officials."

In connection with an agreement concerning the plastics industry, the considerations taken into account by the Rohm & Haas Company and du Pont are indicated in a memorandum written by the latter company in 1936, in which it is stated:

"We discussed the whole situation again. They repeated over and over again that there is not the slightest possibility of the I.C.I.'s coming into the American market, but du Ponts are afraid to write a letter to this effect because in the case of an investigation of their firm by politicians, the politicians might make capital of such a statement, i.e., they might attempt to point out that the world was divided up between I.C.I. and du Ponts.

"I told Mr. Wardenburg that I had implicit faith in all the assurances which they had made to me, but that for my own protection I had to have a letter from du Ponts, in which they can assure us, in one way or another, that the I.C.I. will not take the opportunity to come into this market. After a lengthy discussion of the different ways to accomplish this purpose, it was agreed that Mr. Wardenburg will write a letter saying that while it is true that the I.C.I. under their contract have a right to come into the American market, they [du Ponts] happen to know that the I.C.I.'s development in the methacrylic ester field has taken a direction which is quite different from the one that is being taken by du Ponts and ourselves, so that it will be highly improbable that the I.C.I. will attempt to come into the

U. S. market. I told him that such a letter will be satisfactory."

It is clear that cartel interests fear that the revelation of the provisions of their agreements might impede the functioning of the agreements or perhaps draw down upon them action by public authority. Very often cartel agreements endeavor to discount this possibility in advance. In the case of the agreements between Standard Oil and I. G. Farbenindustrie it is provided that:

"It is our understanding . . . that each party proposes to hold itself willing to take care of any future eventualities in a spirit of mutual helpfulness particularly along the following lines: In the event the performance of these agreements . . . by either party should be hereafter restrained or prevented by operation of any existing or future law, or the beneficial interests of either party be alienated to substantial degree by operation of law or governmental authority, both parties should enter into new negotiations in the spirit of the present agreements and endeavor to adapt their relations to the changed conditions which have arisen."

Because most cartel agreements provide for their resumption at the end of the present war, efforts to rehabilitate world trade may be insuperably handicapped unless prompt and effective action is taken by the government with full knowledge of the existence and character of such cartel agreements. Regardless of the particular form or direction of this nation's trade policies after the war they could not become effective if secret agreements among the large industrial groups of the world contain arrangements which clash with the government's program.

It is well to recall that the provisions of the Versailles Treaty at the end of the first World War which prohibited the manufacture of certain strategic products in Germany were rendered ineffective in many instances. Through foreign subsidiaries and under the cloak of cartel agreements with concerns in the United States and other countries, German producers of military equipment were able to nullify the application of the conditions imposed by the Treaty.

Public authortiy must not be left in the position of having to work in ignorance. Only by compelling the official acknowledgement and registration of the existence and provisions of agreements which affect our foreign and domestic commerce can government acquaint itself with the arrangements which have been made and which affect so vitally national security and national welfare.

During the present war one of the most serious problems with which the fighting services have had to contend on the battle fronts is the frequency of malaria, one of the most widespread diseases in the world. There are two standard remedies for malaria; one is quinine, a natural product obtained from the cinchona trees of Java; the other is atabrine, a synthetic coal-tar product. Because the production and distribution of quinine were controlled by one of the most closely-knit cartels in existence, a shortage developed almost immediately when the Japanese seized Java. The dwindling stockpile of quinine in the United States compelled the government to call upon druggists and housewives alike to turn over whatever small quantities were on hand in order to keep the fighting front supplied.

In the case of atabrine, only one company in the United States had a license to manufacture the drug under the I. G. Farben patents. It required the concerted effort of manufacturers and government to institute expanded production in order to make up deficiencies in quinine supplies. Fortunately, these efforts have met with some success. With regard to the future, however, it must be borne in mind that cartels which are able to control and restrict the output of medical products, in particular those which are so widely needed, as quinine and atabrine, exert a direct influence on the military position of the United States and other countries, as well as upon the general health of the population. The opportunities for abuse which are present in monopolistic control of medical products are obvious. It is equally obvious that this government cannot afford to tolerate them. It would seem a minimum precaution to require that where cartels control the supply, the price, and the distribution of medical products, they should be compelled to record the terms on which control is based, in order that government might in its turn develop adequate safeguards for the general welfare.

I believe it has been clearly demonstrated that certain fundamental decisions affecting our relations with the rest of the world have been formulated and put into effect by private groups without the sanction or knowledge of government. These decisions concerning our strategic materials, industries and trade, our Good Neighbor and our European policies, our disposition of enemy property, considerations of espionage, secrecy and the evasion of our laws, have all been accomplished without the knowledge of our government or its acquiescence.

If cartels are permitted to continue to enter into their secret agreements, then it will be impossible for the peoples of the world to develop mutual understanding or to share industrial experience and progress. Cartels have been a focus of conspiracy and distrust among nations in the past. It is not too much to say that they will form a nucleus of future distrust and intrigue. A world partitioned by cartels breeds economic friction and disunity. We must face the fact that a cartelized postwar world would inevitably be a world of suspicion and of clandestine international intrigue. Full reciprocity in respect of trade and technology can only be founded on mutual confidence and good faith.

There is current a school of thought which believes we must differentiate between good cartels and bad cartels. Do these people still propose to leave the conduct of our foreign economic policy in the hands of private monopolists, with the one caveat that these people be good monopolists and not bad monopolists? With all the best intentions in the world, it is neither the role nor the responsibility of businessmen to determine political questions which can only be resolved by constituted government. This is a responsibility which I believe businessmen should not undertake, and one which I believe that they do not wish to undertake. Even those businessmen who have engaged in these practices would be shocked to realize the implications of their acts. At the time they were operating in this manner they never thought in political terms, but rather in terms of the local market. Once operating in the international market, however, these businessmen found themselves in ambiguous positions where they were forced to make choices which they never contemplated. What would they do when confronted with the problem of choosing between national policy as it should be and their own private interests? It would seem, from the standpoint of public interest, that when questions of national concern arise they should be handled by properly constituted government authority.

American businessmen have not realized the significance of the relationship between their foreign cartel partners and the foreign governments involved. I doubt that they knew, for example, that the following statement was made by Mr. Meinhardt of Osram, a member of the international lamp cartel: "An international cartel has no right of existence and a German businessman has no right to become a member of such a cartel if this cartel is acting against the common interests of Germany."

The attitude of American businessmen is typified in the following statement by an executive of the General Motors Company: "an international business operating throughout the world, should conduct its operations in strictly business terms, without regard to the political beliefs of its management, or the political beliefs of the country in which it is operating."

All American businessmen and the Congress particularly should weigh with care the type of thinking which results from a cartelized economy such as Germany's. Carl Duisberg, formerly chairman of the board of I. G. Farbenindustrie, expressed succinctly the philosophy of Germany's cartel system when he said, in 1932: "The narrowness of the national economic territory must be overcome by trans-national economic territories . . . For a final settlement of the problem of Europe . . . a close economic combine must be formed from Bordeaux to Odessa as the backbone of Europe." The ultimate consequences of such cartel aims have been reckoned across the council tables of Munich and the battlefields of Europe and Asia.

14

Freedom or Control?

All of us want our country to be strong and prosperous after this war is won. In attaining strength and prosperity, foreign trade will play an important part. Manufactured goods will leave the shores of this country and will find their way through the miracle of new forms of transportation, as well as on the tramp steamer, to the four corners of the world. Raw materials, and finished products as well, will come from these same four corners into the hands of the American consumer. The foreign trade of this country will be measured in billions of dollars. And our nation will take its place and play its part in what we believe can be a healthy world economy.

I do not think that there is any basic difference of opinion in this country as to the importance of our foreign trade. There appears to be some difference of views, however, as to how our foreign trade shall be conducted in the post-war world. It is argued that since Europe has a cartel system, if we wish to carry on trade or commerce with Europe or in the world, we must permit our foreign businesses to become cartelized. We are told, in short, that we must join hands with the cartels if we are to engage in foreign trade. Most of the people who make this argument do so regretfully. They know that the Sherman Antitrust Act, which prohibits restraints on both domestic and foreign trade or commerce, has reflected the free enterprise spirit of this country for more than fifty years. They know that the people of this country are unalterably opposed to a cartel system under which either the government or one's competitors can determine what may be manufactured, how much can be made, and what price may be charged. They know that you cannot have a democratic system if enterprise is to be subjected either to government bureaucracy or to the rule of private trade councils. Nevertheless, these people, seeing a cartelized world around us, believe that much as we may dislike it, we cannot conduct foreign trade unless we join hands with the cartels.

There is a small minority in this country, of course, which has always opposed our own free enterprise system. If these people could manage it, they would have the economy of this country run by enlightened and benevolent monopolists. These people make the argument, not at all regretfully, that we must join hands with foreign cartels. They know that once we have joined hands with foreign cartels, we will have opened the door to monopoly at home, and that is what they want.

Let me venture a prediction. This country will engage in foreign trade and commerce on a scale never before imagined, and we are not going to join hands with any foreign cartels. There will be a drive to get us into the foreign cartels; that drive in fact is now going on. It will fail. It will fail for two good reasons. The first of these is that our foreign trade would not be helped in the least if we joined with the cartels. The second and even more important reason is that this country is in no mood to give up an American way of life because Europe believes in cartels.

We have been willing to subject ourselves to all kinds of governmental controls over American business in order to win this war. When the war is over, these controls must go, and as soon as possible. We are not going to keep these controls either in the hands of the government or in the hands of a few private individuals. We are not going to imitate the very foreign economic system which we have defeated.

The monopolist tells us that European industry is cartelized and that it will remain so after this war is over. What kind of wishful thinking makes the monopolist so sure of that? I do not believe that after this war is over the French or the Belgians will wish to embrace an economic system which took their basic industries and put them into the hands of an international set of cartelists dominated by the Germans. I do not believe that the British will wish to encourage a system which in March 1939 gave birth to the announcement between the Federation of British Industries and the German Reichsgruppe Industrie that the two groups would eliminate competition between British and German industries, would fix prices, and would seek the aid of their governments against the industry of any third country, clearly meaning the United States, which did not join in this limitation of production plan. Great Britain needed its own full production in those days, and American production as well. I do not believe, for that matter, that the British will wish to have an economic system which has made the British consumer pay high prices and has restricted production in both Great Britain and the Dominions.

It is clear, of course, that in each country of the world, there are a few monopolists who will benefit from the cartel system. We have them in our country also. But we are not going to let these few determine our own economic life, and we should not let them control our attitude or actions in Europe. Certainly it is too early to predict that Europe will remain cartelized after this war. I think it is not unlikely that the consumers of Europe will decide they have had enough of that system and will demand a change.

But no matter what Europe does, our foreign trade will not be helped in the least by our joining foreign cartels. The very reverse is true. The way to kill American foreign trade is to have American producers enter into international cartels. One reason for the current drive to get American firms into foreign cartels is precisely that. There are a few monopolists who do not look with favor upon sales by American firms in the rest of the world. They are terrified that our mass production methods may benefit consumers in the rest of the world. They will not be able to maintain their own prices if this should occur. Their invitation for us to join them in cartel agreements is not an invitation to engage in trade or commerce; it is an invitation to discover upon what terms and conditions we will keep our trade at home.

The record is very clear. A small number of powerful American firms entered into illegal cartel agreements before the war, particularly in the halcyon days of the twenties. These were agreements to restrict American exports. Typically, the American firms agreed not only not to export themselves but wherever possible to keep other American firms from exporting. These agreements occurred in synthetic nitrogen, aluminum, magnesium, optical glass, electric lamps, pharmaceuticals, plastics, chemicals and a host of other items. It is quixotic to think of these agreements as having promoted foreign trade; their whole purpose was to prevent it. Where was our foreign trade when these firms agreed to turn over the Latin American market in pharmaceuticals to the Germans? What foreign trade was being promoted when we agreed not to export to Great

Britain more than a limited quantity of magnesium? The underlying philosophy of these agreements was that if the foreign firms would stay out of the American market, we would stay out of the foreign market.

There is no mystery about this. The monopolists know it very well as do the other American companies, large and small, who were not permitted to export because if they did so, they would interfere with the arrangements to keep trade and commerce from flowing in either direction across the borders of this country. The reasoning is clearly set forth by an official of an American company in explaining why his company cannot export:

". . . you spoke of a possible license from the G.E. to export lamps to certain countries. I don't know whether I explained the situation to you, but the fact is that in the world at large, the more important electrical interests, such as the G.E., Siemens of Germany, Phillips of Holland, etc., are closely bound together in a cartel with the result that they have entered into binding agreements, apportioning world markets between the respective companies. Accordingly you can see that if the G.E. broke their agreement and allowed us to export into a foreign country which was assigned under the cartel agreement to a European manufacturer, that European manufacturer would have a claim to enter the American market in competition with us and probably could not be restrained from doing so. This is something which would probably not be to our advantage."

One might as well urge that a railway wreck promotes transportation as to urge that a cartel agreement promotes trade.

The cartelist lives in a land of make-believe. I do not suppose that we can object to anyone having his own private fairy tale, but this kind of fairy tale can be dangerous to the future peace and security of this country. It is a self-perpetuating fairy tale. It is founded on economic maladjustments and it tends to prolong these maladjustments by collecting a hidden tax from consumers and by donating the proceeds to monopolists who have no incentive to change their ways. The consequences can be disastrous in both the military and the political sphere. As for our own economic life, international cartels breed domestic monopolies. Their final result is complete government control and management of business.

The cartelist appears to believe that the way to engage in foreign trade is to have a conference—a kind of Alice in Wonderland mad tea party. At this conference the world is divided up; markets are allocated; and, if he is fortunate, an American enterpriser will be given some business. At the end of the conference he can telephone his office and say "Men, we have been given the Shangri-La market; it's all ours." Sometimes the cartelist sounds as though he were too lazy to attend the conference himself. He wants his Government to go for him. He wants the Government to tell him what to do, what markets he can have, and what he can sell. One gets the impression that foreign trade is conducted in an armchair, that it is better if you can get the Government to do it for you, and that it does not make much difference what you have to sell.

This kind of thinking is dangerous. It is a denial of the principle of private property with the profit reward for private initiative and risk taking. Foreign trade presents special problems, but it is none the less true in foreign as well as in domestic trade that if you want to sell you have to make a product the consumer wants to buy. In the development of the foreign market there is no panacea, no easy substitute for ingenuity and efficiency. We cannot expect the foreign consumer to adjust his desires to whatever it is we want to sell. We have to make the kind of a product he wants to buy. The truth of the matter is that many of the large concerns that have made cartel agreements have not been particularly anxious to sell in the foreign market. They have been more anxious to keep independent enterprise in this country from gaining access to foreign markets than they were to sell themselves. As a consequence we must frankly admit that in many industries, American enterprise has not shown the competitive alertness it has at home. If it does not show competitive alertness, it does not deserve the business. And you cannot find a substitute for competitive alertness in an armchair cartel conference or even in an intergovernmental cartel conference.

The cartel conference is a kind of legislature, imposing hidden taxes on consumers and bestowing bounties on others, without the necessity for disclosure or responsibility to any electorate. It is truly a method of imposing taxation without representation. This is true in every cartel case. Some time ago it was fashionable to scoff at international relief or development projects as being international WPAs. Americans were asked rhetorically whether they wished to take care of inhabitants on some other portion of the globe. But no relief scheme has ever been imagined, and no one would dare to present it, which could begin to compare with the international relief societies maintained for themselves by the international cartels. Gigantic sums are drained from the American consumer each year and given outright to domestic monopolists and to foreign companies operating in protected markets. When it is urged that American companies should be allowed to join with foreign cartels in order to promote foreign trade, it should be remembered that what is there called foreign trade is in reality a gigantic relief enterprise supported by the American consumer. I can illustrate this with an example taken from one of our earliest cartel cases.

The story begins prior to the First World War with the

discovery and development in Germany of a way of making synthetic nitrate of soda by taking nitrogen out of the air. Prior to that discovery, the world was dependent upon Chile for its nitrate of soda for use in both fertilizer and the making of munitions. The discovery of this new way of making nitrate of soda changed the history of the world for it made it possible for the Germans to wage war without depending upon a raw material to be found only in the Western Hemisphere. It is probable that if synthetic nitrogen had not been discovered, the Germans could not have been able to go to war.

The Allies at that time were dependent upon Chilean nitrate of soda, and as a military matter, this dependence made the Allied position in the first years of the war exceedingly precarious. The Germans knew that Great Britain could not stay in the war for any considerable length of time if it were cut off from its only source of nitrogen, and accordingly in 1917, the Germans set up a blockade outside of Valparaiso. The first attempt of the British to break this blockade was unsuccessful, but the blockade was finally removed as a result of the battle of the Falkland Islands when Admiral Von Spee was defeated. As an economic matter, this dependence of the Allies upon Chilean nitrate of soda was, of course, good for Chile. The United States in 1917 and 1918 purchased almost four million tons of nitrate from Chile; we paid on the average of about $82.50 per ton. At one time, the price rose to $150.00 per ton. In those days, Chile had a unique product, a natural monopoly, and we had to pay for it. The First World War gave to Chile the chance to receive large revenues on a valuable asset, but the First World War also created a situation where in the days to come that asset would depreciate enormously.

The asset of Chilean nitrate of soda was depreciated enormously because all of the important countries of the world, including our own, began to produce synthetic nitrate of soda. Chile no longer had a natural monopoly safe from effective competition. The producers of synthetic nitrate of soda began to compete with each other and with the Chileans. In order to remove this competition they formed a cartel.

The cartel was formed in 1926 and by 1938 it had reached its full growth. The cartel was dominated in Europe by the so-called DEN group, composed of Imperial Chemical Industries, Ltd. for the British, Stickstoff-Syndikat, controlled by I. G. Farbenindustrie for the Germans, and Norsk Hydro for the Norwegians. The European end of the cartel formed an international company in Switzerland to handle the cartel affairs, and thus to represent the thirty-five principal European producers. By special agreements the cartel was extended to cover the Chilean producers of natural nitrate, and I am sorry to say, the important American producers as well. The cartel was an international combination to restrict production, maintain prices and to allocate territories. The world was divided up into special zones of influence; quotas were assigned, and sales in forbidden areas or above the allowed quota resulted in the assessment of penalties. Mexico, for instance, was allocated to the German producers. The American producers were required to refrain from exporting to certain areas. The Barrett Company could not sell substantial quantities of nitrate of soda in foreign markets reserved for the Chilean producers. Du Pont was kept from selling a nitrogenous product in the Philippine Islands. This was not an international trade agreement; as is true with all cartel agreements, this was an agreement to restrict trade.

The cartel agreements covered the American market. Imports by a foreign company to this country had to be included in determining whether that company had exceeded its quota of the world market. American companies were restricted in their exports and to some extent in their production. And sales in the American market, whether for Chilean, European or American producers were at agreed upon prices. An elaborate system of distribution was worked out and adhered to so that these agreed upon prices could be maintained down through the wholesalers and retailers. The cartel thus reached down and touched the American farmer buying in the country store.

Now nitrate of soda is important to the American farmer as are the other fertilizer nitrogen products which were covered by this cartel. In 1937, approximately 700,000 tons of nitrate of soda were imported from Chile for distribution to the American farmer. If there is a cartel in fertilizer nitrogen, it is the American farmer who pays. And he has paid in millions of dollars—a hidden tax to the foreign and domestic producers.

Production was restricted and prices were fixed by this cartel. Some of the higher prices went to Chile; some of them went to our own producers and abroad. The consumer, who in this country happened to be the American farmer, paid a tax in the form of higher prices to keep this cartel going. He did not know he was paying this tax. He did not have the opportunity to elect a representative who might have been for or against this tax. And yet, out of every dollar the farmer paid, a part of it was an involuntary offering to the cartel.

And what was the good from all of this? A hidden tax was collected; purchasing power was destroyed. And all of this was done so that productive capacity could go unused. Out of the hidden tax paid by the American farmer, only a part of it went to the Chilean companies; a good deal of it went to American and European producers.

Whenever the argument is made that a cartel supports a distress industry, the complete answer is that it would be cheaper and better to make an outright gift, raised, if necessary, by lawful general taxation through the Congress. It would be cheaper because consumers would not be required to pay an additional amount to those who are not distressed as they have to do when the cartel keeps the general price up. It would be better because if it were a gift, it would not be raised from only one group of consumers, as in this case, the farmers. It would be better because the contributors to the gift fund would have some chance to know what they were doing and to decide whether they wanted to do it. Nor would the gift be as likely to disappear under the burden of an inefficient method of production as is the case with the hidden tax which is collected every year and which imposes no incentive upon the monopolist to change his ways. You cannot expect the monopolist to change his ways when he can collect a hidden tax every year. No doubt after this war, it will be argued that synthetic nitrogen capacity should go unused by agreement between the large companies. We should remember that if this is done, as with all cartel agreements, there is a hidden and unlawful tax; in this case it would be the American farmers who would pay.

I do not revive this synthetic nitrogen story in order to make charges, but merely as a specific illustration of the way cartels operate. The actual cases are the best answers to the argument that cartels promote trade. The synthetic nitrogen cartel was typical in many ways. The particular occasion for the birth of this cartel was the development of a synthetic process which threatened to destroy the capital value of a natural product. After this war, there will be many new processes whose existence will destroy old capital values and which can be looked upon either as keys to open the doors of new opportunities or as occasions for restrictive agreements. The synthetic nitrogen cartel brought together producers fearful of each other's productive capacity. As is true in almost every important cartel, the restrictive agreements might have had important military consequences, even though many of the private producers were only thinking in terms of a peace-time market. And finally, this foreign cartel, as is so frequently the case, bred a domestic cartel.

The effect is far-reaching both politically and economically. You can never deal with just one cartel separate from the others because the cartel world is an intricate and interrelated maze. Thus the foreign participants in the nitrogen cartel include the German I. G. Farbenindustrie and the British Imperial Chemical Industries—each a member of a variety of world dividing cartels. The American producers, whether they knew it or not, were entering into an international game to divide markets in which every market and every type of product was involved if the full scope of the cartel agreements of their partners were revealed. They were dealing in secret international diplomacy.

In many cases they were in reality dealing with foreign governments, despite the fact that it has not been the policy of this country to have the conduct of our foreign affairs in private hands. Since 1799 an Act of Congress has prohibited every citizen of the United States, without the permission of the Government, from carrying on any written or verbal correspondence or intercourse with any foreign government with an intent to influence the measures or conduct of any foreign government in relation to any disputes or controversies with the United States. Quite apart from whether this criminal statute is applicable, its spirit would deny to any citizen the right to barter away the trade of the United States by agreement with a foreign government.

One need only think of the possible disastrous effects of permitting Germany to build up a monopoly position in Latin

America. The economic effects grow like a snow-ball. Thus in the instance of the synthetic nitrogen cartel, the American consumer lost purchasing power; that meant that American producers could sell less and could therefore buy less. The Chileans received only a portion of the amount of money taken out of purchasing power, but the related cartels operate in Chile, such as the chemical cartel of which both Imperial Chemical Industries and du Pont's are members. And these cartels do the same thing to Chile that the synthetic nitrogen cartel did to us. Economic life is so related today that you cannot restrict one part and not have almost endless repercussions. For instance, if American movies should be kept out of foreign areas, the effect is immediate on all kinds of American products which are advertised continually through the medium of the motion picture. If the motion picture producers enter into a cartel agreement, they are restricting a good deal of American trade in addition to their own.

What then is the solution? There is no solution if the problem is how can you have American firms enter into foreign cartel agreements but not restrict American trade and commerce. It is surely no solution to say that in the future we will have the governments enter into cartel agreements for us. As an economic matter, it makes no difference whether an agreement to restrict trade is private or governmental. As a political matter, I would agree that if we are going to have such agreements, with their widespread economic diseases, they had better be the responsibility of the government, if only because the government which makes such agreements can be changed by the voters. But I would suggest that effective governmental control over such agreements would require such a degree of interference and surveillance over private industry as to place in great jeopardy our own free enterprise-private property system. The history of attempts to control cartels by legalizing and controlling them is not particularly inspiring. Germany is one example.

There is not any one solution because there is not just one problem. There are many things which must and can be done if this country is to encourage foreign trade.

First, we must encourage domestic research. Any country which wishes to engage in trade and commerce in the future industrial era must develop its own laboratories and encourage its own domestic research. It has sometimes been suggested that the reason why some of our larger American companies entered into agreements to stay out of important markets such as Latin America was because such was the price they had to pay to get the benefits of European research. It has sometimes even been suggested that we have been dependent upon European research acquired in this manner for many of the important developments which have helped us in this war.

There will probably always be a certain amount of obscurity about this claim that we are dependent upon European research. The files of some of the Antitrust Division cases, however, indicate that even though German firms may have been bound under their agreements to make their research available to their American friends, in many important instances they did not do so. In any event, I think we would agree that it is of the utmost importance that American firms be able to stand on their own feet, and that they should not be dependent upon research from abroad. It has been quite natural, of course, for European research to be in advance of our own in some fields. But failure to develop our own laboratories and our own scientists would be criminal negligence.

I suggest that we ought to have an impartial and searching survey begun as soon as possible as to American research facilities and the state of American research. This is not a matter which concerns only our foreign trade. It goes to the very heart of our future domestic well-being.

Of course, I do not mean to suggest that we should cut ourselves off from European research. There is every reason to believe that research in the future will be truly international in the sense that a partial discovery in England will be supplemented by work done in France or in this country. Possibly some inter-governmental agency can be developed which will act as a kind of international clearing house in order to speed the development of common research carried on in separate areas. It is likely that private institutions in this country and the government itself, as suggested by Senator Kilgore, could aid in the performing of this function. If a study were made of our own domestic research facilities, I would expect that out of that study a recommendation might well come to set up some kind of an international clearing house for research.

There is a further step we can take. The research which has been developed in Germany during the last ten years under the Nazi regime is research which in right belongs to the people of the United Nations. It was Nazi government sponsored research used for the purpose of making war upon us. It is research which should now be put to use for the general good of mankind. It should not be considered as belonging to private hands either in Germany or elsewhere. The United Nations should make sure that steps are taken to make available this research so that it can be used generally.

Second, we must remove, through inter-governmental action, the waste and misuse of resources which occur when industries cannot compete and are artificially maintained. It will be much cheaper for this country to offer transitional credit to be used to develop new industries than to continue paying hidden taxes which don't accomplish anything. We should set up an international mechanism whereby substantial credit can be made available to other countries upon such terms as will encourage the readjustment of the use of their resources so that these resources can be employed, without the crutch of a trade barrier, in the free trade of the world. Consistent with this aim, we can urge also the adoption of minimum wage and health standards so that labor exploitation does not become the means of providing a hidden subsidy for industry in countries having substandard labor conditions.

Third, it is, of course, imperative that this country make known its determination to encourage foreign trade and to make it possible for American firms, large and small, to bring their goods to the consumers who will buy. Through vigorous antitrust action, we can break up the activities of a great number of foreign cartels. And American firms are perfectly capable of engaging in vigorous competition with the old monopolistic companies of Europe. Where American industry is competitive at home, such as the automobile industry, there is no way a foreign company effectively can keep out American goods, and foreign consumers would be the first to object if that were tried. It is the industries which are monopolistically dominated at home which seem to have the greatest difficulty. I suspect, however, that in those industries there are smaller firms who will be glad to have the opportunity of selling abroad.

Fourth, we should stand ready to help create an international forum to which countries denied access to raw materials or allowed to purchase them only on the basis of monopolistic prices can go to present their case. This does not mean that we should take part in any international control of business, but it does mean that for those few areas where monopolies continue to persist, we must create a world where there is a remedy within the structure of the peace. Many of these raw materials no longer have their former importance. Poetic justice may come to rubber, quinine and eventually to diamonds. Persistence in monopoly prices usually stimulates the development of a substitute. The international forum which I urge will probably not have to hear too many cases. The power of competition has grown more powerful during the war because of the development of myriads of substitutes for the key raw materials.

The opportunities are tremendous. The tools needed for the job are the productive facilities and materials which we will have in abundance. We can play our part with energy and initiative; we would not have it otherwise. We believe in competition, and we are ready to compete. We are ready to engage wholeheartedly in rebuilding a world of peace in which every man and every country can have a stake. We know that we cannot maintain, let alone advance our standard of living save upon the basis of an active and expanding international trade. Our expanding trade will enlarge the area of the interests which we have in common with other peoples, and for us, as well as for them, will narrow the intensity of our differences. And we will have played our part in foreign trade in such a way as to preserve the symbol of our political and economic democracy.

APPENDIX I

Recent Cases

The most effective weapon presently available for combatting the influence of monopoly and cartel-minded international groups is vigorous enforcement of the antitrust laws. Congress has recognized that the natural effect of competition is to increase commerce—to extinguish or prevent the free play of competition is to hinder commerce. As was stated by Mr. Chief Justice Stone in the *Trenton Potteries* case:

"Whatever difference of opinion there may be among economists as to the social and economic desirability of an unrestrained competitive system, it cannot be doubted that the Sherman Law and the judicial decisions interpreting it are based upon the assumption that the public interest is best protected from the evils of monopoly and price control by the maintenance of competition."

By passage of the antitrust laws, Congress has expressed the American policy of free competition not only in interstate trade and commerce but also in our foreign trade and commerce. The provisions of Section 73 of the Wilson Tariff Act further exemplify this doctrine with specific reference to imports to this country. Section 11 of the Panama Canal Act prohibits passage through the Panama Canal of ships owned or operated by persons doing business in violation of the antitrust laws. Thus, the practices of foreign cartels, involving elimination of competition and collectivization of industry, are inconsonant with the basic concepts of our antitrust laws and national economic policy. The type of arrangements which are the cornerstone of European cartelization, such as agreements dividing markets, allocating customers, controlling production and prices, and apportioning business have all been long declared to be in violation of our antitrust statutes by the courts.

By and large, the antitrust laws can be effectively applied to combat restraints upon the domestic and foreign commerce of the United States whether the practices, agreements or conspiracies complained of have their inception in this country or elsewhere.

It has become an accepted principle of law that acts done or agreements entered into in a foreign jurisdiction, even though lawful there, may be prosecuted or enjoined in this country where the effect or result of such acts or agreements is a violation of our laws. This principle has been applied in antitrust cases, and agreements which restrain our trade with foreign nations have been uniformly declared illegal. Our courts may control foreign citizens or corporations operating wholly in foreign territory, where their operations extend into the domestic and foreign commerce of this country, just as we may undoubtedly control the activities of our own citizens and our own corporations which impinge upon our domestic and foreign trade and commerce.

The mere fact that a combination is formed in a foreign country does not prevent the application of our laws where it affects the foreign commerce of this country and is put into operation here. Conversely, combinations or agreements entered into in the United States and adversely affecting the foreign trade of this country are subject to the antitrust laws even though the acts done to effectuate the restraints are performed outside this country. It is recognized that some cartel arrangements are instigated by or under cover of foreign governmental authority, but unless the cartel arrangements complained of are solely participated in by the foreign government, the situation is not altered.

While a foreign sovereign may have immunity from suit, such immunity does not apply to private individuals or organizations even though they may be acting pursuant to the laws of their own country, or as agents for their government or though a foreign government may have a substantial financial interest in the challenged organization and activities.

The practical difficulty of acquiring personal jurisdiction over some of the foreign individual or corporate participants in a cartel which affects our foreign or domestic commerce is often confused with the question of whether or not a violation of our antitrust laws is involved. This, however, is a technical problem depending upon an aggregation of facts rather than a question of substantive law involved in restraints upon commerce.

The following is a list of antitrust cartel cases instituted by the Department of Justice since 1937:

Aircraft Accessories: Bendix Aviation Corporation, et al.; complaint filed November 19, 1942; postponement of trial requested by War and Navy Departments.

Alkali: United States Alkali Export Assn., Inc., et al.; complaint filed March 16, 1944; argument had May 10, 1944 on motions to dismiss.

Aluminum: Aluminum Company of America, et al.; petition filed April 23, 1937; judgment denying Government relief filed July 23, 1942; on appeal.

Chemicals: Imperial Chemical Industries, Ltd., et al.; complaint filed January 6, 1944.

Chemicals and Petroleum (Including Synthetic Rubber): Standard Oil Company (N. J.), et al.; complaint filed March 25, 1942; consent decree entered March 25, 1942; supplemental judgment filed April 7, 1943. Information filed and pleas of nolo contendere on March 25, 1942; fines levied totaled $50,000.

Dyestuffs: Allied Chemical & Dye Corp., et al.; indictment returned May 14, 1942; Attorney General acquiesced in postponement of trial until it will not interfere with defendant's war production. General Dyestuff Corp., et al.; indictment returned December 19, 1941; pending on preliminary motions.

Fertilizer: American Potash & Chemical Corp., et al.; complaint filed May 15, 1940; consent decree entered May 21, 1940; Chilean Nitrate Sales Corp., et al.; indictment returned September 1, 1939; dismissed as to 18 defendants June 3, 1941 to August 28, 1942; pleas of nolo contendere by 6 defendants August 28, 1942; fines levied totalled $35,000. Allied Chemical & Dye Corp., et al.; complaint and consent decree entered May 29, 1941. Imperial Chemical Industries (N. Y.), Ltd., et al.; complaint and consent decree February 17 and 18, 1942. Mutual Chemical Company of America, et al.; indictment returned June 26, 1942; Attorney General acquiesced in requests by War and Navy Departments for postponement of trial. Synthetic Nitrogen Products Corp., et al.; complaint and consent decree, September 5, 1941.

Fluorescent Lamps: General Electric Company, et al.; complaint filed December 9, 1942; Attorney General acquiesced in postponement of trial requested by War and Navy Departments.

Fuel Injection Equipment: American Bosch Corp. and Donald P. Hess; complaint and consent decree, December 29, 1942.

Glass Bulbs: Corning Glass Works, et al.; indictment returned August 28, 1940; pleas of nolo contendere and fines totalling $47,000 September 9, 1941.

Gyroscopic Instruments: The Sperry Corporation, et al.; complaint and consent decree entered September 1, 1942.

Hormones: Ciba Pharmaceutical Products, Inc., et al.; information filed and pleas of nolo contendere, December 17, 1941; fines of $18,000. Roche-Organon, Inc., and Elmer H. Bobst; information filed and pleas of nolo contendere, December 17, 1941; fines of $6,000. Schering Corporation, et al.; information filed and pleas of nolo contendere, December 17, 1941; fines of $24,000; complaint and consent decree entered same day. Swiss Bank Corporation; complaint and consent decree, December 17, 1941. Julius Weltzien and Schering Corporation; information filed and pleas of nolo contendere, December 17, 1941; fines of $6,000.

Incandescent Lamps: General Electric Company, et al.; complaint filed January 27, 1941; Attorney General acquiesced in postponement of trial requested by War and Navy Departments.

Magnesite Brick: Harbison-Walker Refractories Company, et al.; indictment returned January 20, 1941; pleas of nolo contendere and fines of $76,500, July 22, 1941; pending as to Veitscher Magnesitwerke Aktiengesellschaft and Magnesit Co., Ltd., whose motion to vacate services of summons has been referred to a special master, also as to Magnesit Industrie Aktiengesellschaft.

Magnesium: Aluminum Company of America, et al.; complaint filed; consent decree entered April 15, 1942; indictment returned January 30, 1941; pleas of nolo contendere,

April 15, 1942, and fines of $104,993. To be set for trial as to I. G. Farben and Dietrich Schmitz. American Magnesium Corporation, et al.; indictment returned January 30, 1941; pleas of nolo contendere and fines of $15,003, April 15, 1942; case to be set for trial as to I. G. Farben and Gustav Pistor. Dow Chemical Company, et al.; indictment returned January 30, 1941; pleas of nolo contendere and fines of $20,004, April 15, 1942; to be set for trial as to I. G. Farben.

Matches: Diamond Match Company, et al.; complaint filed May 1, 1944.

Military Optical Instruments: Bausch & Lomb Optical Company, et al.; indictment returned March 26, 1940; pleas of nolo contendere and fines of $41,000, May 27, 1940 and March 5, 1941; pending as to Carl Zeiss (a German firm). Complaint filed July 9, 1940, and consent decree entered same day as to all defendants except Carl Zeiss.

Molybdenum: Climax Molybdenum Company, et al.; complaint filed August 19, 1942 and consent decree entered August 21, 1942.

News Reporting: The Associated Press, et al.; complaint filed August 28, 1942; Decree for Government January 13, 1944; appeal of defendants docketed in Supreme Court, April 13, 1944.

Newsprint Paper: Crown Zellerbach Corporation, et al.; indictment returned July 12, 1939; 6 defendants pleaded nolo contendere and were fined $30,000, May 2, 1941; remaining defendants dismissed.

Pharmaceutical Products: Alba Pharmaceutical Company, Inc., et al.; information filed, pleas of nolo contendere, and fines of $26,000, September 5, 1941; complaint filed and consent decree entered same day. The Bayer Company, Inc., et al.; complaint filed and consent decree entered, September 5,

1941. Merck & Company, Inc., et al.; complaint filed October 28, 1943; Government moved to join the Alien Property Custodian as party plaintiff, May 8, 1944.

Photographic Materials: General Aniline & Film Corporation, et al.; indictment returned December 19, 1941; pending on preliminary motions. Dietrich A. Schmitz, et al.; indictment returned December 19, 1941; pending on preliminary motions.

Plastics: E. I. du Pont de Nemours & Company, et al.; indictment returned August 10, 1942; Attorney General acquiesced in postponement of trial requested by War and Navy Departments.

Quebracho: The Forestal Land, Timber and Railways, Ltd., et al.; complaint filed December 20, 1943; pending on preliminary motions. The Tannin Corporation, et al.; indictment returned November 24, 1942; pleas of nolo contendere and fines of $59,003, January 12, 1943 and April 19, 1943; dismissed as to the remaining defendants, August 24, 1943.

Titanium Compounds: National Lead Company, et al.; indictment returned June 28, 1943; case set for trial on October 3, 1944; complaint filed July 1, 1944.

Tungsten Carbide: General Electric Company, et al.; indictment returned August 30, 1940; superseding indictment returned October 21, 1941; Attorney General acquiesced in postponement of trial requested by War and Navy Departments.

APPENDIX II

Bibliography

Arnold, Thurman W., *The Bottlenecks of Business*, New York, 1940.

Ballande, Laurence, *Essai d'etude Monographique et Statistique sur les Ententes Economiques Internationales*, Paris, 1936.

Boehm, Franz, *Wettbewerb und Monopolkampf*, Berlin, 1933.

Borkin, Joseph and Welsh, Charles A., *Germany's Master Plan*, New York, 1943.

Burns, Arthur R., *The Decline of Competition*, New York, 1936.

Clark, John B., *Control of Trusts*, New York, 1912.

Conte, Roger, *Report on International Industrial Ententes*, Paris, 1927. (International Chamber of Commerce Brochure No. 46).

Domeratzky, Louis, *The International Cartel Movement*, Washington, 1928. (U. S. Department of Commerce, Bureau of Foreign and Domestic Commerce, Trade Information Bulletin No. 556).

Edwards, Corwin, *Economic and Political Aspects of International Cartels*, Washington, 1944.

Elliott, William Y., and May, Elizabeth S., and Rowe, I. W. F., and others, *International Control in the Nonferrous Metals*, New York, 1937.

Ely, Richard T., *Monopoly and Trusts*, New York, 1912.

Ertel, Erich, *Internationale Kartelle und Konzerne der Industrie*, Stuttgart, 1930.

Fetter, Frank A., *The Masquerade of Monopoly*, New York, 1931.

Friedlaender, Heinrich, *Die Rechtslage der Konzerne und Kartelle in Europa*, Zurich, 1938.

Greaves, H. R. G., *Raw Materials and International Control*, London, 1936.

Hamilton, Walton H., *The Pattern of Competition*, New York, 1940.

Hantos, Elemer, *Mitteleuropaeische Kartelle im Dienste des Industriellen Zusammenschlusses*, Berlin, 1931.

Hexner, Ervin, *The International Steel Cartel*, Chapel Hill, 1943.

Hodson, H. V., *Slump and Recovery, 1929-37*, London, New York, Toronto, 1938.

Holland, W. L., Editor, *Commodity Control in the Pacific Area*, Stanford, 1935.

International Labor Office, *Intergovernmental Commodity Control Agreements*, Montreal, 1943.

Jenks, Jeremiah W., *The Trust Problem*, New York, 1929.

Johnson, Eric, *America Unlimited*, New York, 1944.

Kyrpriotis, M., *Les Cartels Internationaux*, Paris, 1936.

Laidler, Harry W., *Concentration of Control in American Industry*, New York, 1931.

League of Nations Council, Report of the Committee for the Study of Raw Materials, *Official Journal*, December, 1937.

League of Nations, *Economic Aspects of Several International Industrial Agreements*. Geneva, 1930.

Levi, Edward H., "Cartels and the War" in *War and the Law*, edited by B. W. Puttkammer, Chicago, 1944.

Liefmann, Robert, *Cartels, Concerns and Trusts*, London, 1932.

MacGregor, David H., *Industrial Combinations*, London, 1938.

MacGregor, David H., *International Cartels*, Geneva, 1927.

Marquand, Hilary A., *Dynamics of Industrial Combinations*, New York, 1931.

Meyers, Ernest S., & Lewis, Seymour D., "The Patent 'Franchise' and the Antitrust Laws," *Georgetown Law Journal*, December 1941 and January 1942.

Michels, Rudolf, *Cartels, Combines and Trusts in Postwar Germany*, London, 1928.

Notz, William F., *Representative International Cartels, Combines, and Trusts*, Washington, 1929. (U. S. Department of Commerce, Bureau of Foreign and Domestic Commerce, Trade Promotion Series No. 81).

Oualid, William, *International Raw Materials Cartels*, Paris, 1938. (League of Nations, International Studies Conference.)

Piotrowski, Roman, *Cartels and Trusts*, London, 1933.

Plummer, Alfred, *International Combines in Modern Industry*, London, 1938

Pribram, Karl, *Cartel Problems*, Washington, 1935.

Rappeport, Samuel, *Les Cartels en Pologne*, Nancy, 1935.

Razous, Paul, *Cartels, Trusts, et Divers Ententes de Producteurs*, Paris, 1935.

Reimann, Guenter, *Patents for Hitler*, New York, 1943.

Robbins, Lionel, *Economic Planning and International Order*, London, 1937.

Rowe, I. W. F., *Markets and Men*, New York, Cambridge, 1936.

Staley, Eugene, *Raw Materials in Peace and War*, New York, 1937.

Tschernoff, J., *Ententes Economiques et Financieres*, Paris, 1933.

United States Congress, *Hearings Before the Temporary National Economic Committee, 76th Congress, 3rd Session on Public Resolution No. 113, Investigation of Concentration of Economic Power*, Testimony of Theodore J. Kreps, Part 25, Washington, 1940.

United States Congress, *Hearings Before the Senate Committee on Patents, 77th Congress, 2nd Session on S-2303, Patents*. Washington, 1942.

Veblen, Thorstein, *Imperial Germany and the Industrial Revolution*, New York, 1942.

Voorhis, Jerry, *Beyond Victory*, New York, 1944.

Wallace, Benjamin Bruce and Edminster, Lynn Ramsey, *International Control of Raw Materials*, Washington, 1930.

Warriner, Dorun, *Combines and Rationalization in Germany*, London, 1931.

Watkins, Myron W., *Industrial Combinations and Public Policy*, Boston, 1927.

Wheeler, Leslie, "Agricultural Surpluses in the Postwar World," *Foreign Affairs*, v. 20, 1941.

Wiedenfeld, Kurt, *Cartels and Combines*, Geneva, 1927. (League of Nations publication.)

Index

www.ingramcontent.com/pod-product-compliance
Lightning Source LLC
LaVergne TN
LVHW090315210926
848480LV00001B/259